The Software Programmer
Basis of common protocols and procedures

S. Mathioudakis

authorHOUSE

AuthorHouse™ UK
1663 Liberty Drive
Bloomington, IN 47403 USA
www.authorhouse.co.uk
Phone: UK TFN: 0800 0148641 (Toll Free inside the UK)
       UK Local: (02) 0369 56322 (+44 20 3695 6322 from outside the UK)

Published by AuthorHouse 09/12/2024

ISBN: 979-8-8230-8987-6 (sc)
ISBN: 979-8-8230-8988-3 (e)

Library of Congress Control Number: 2024919419

CONTENTS

Foreword.. vii

Preface ix

Part 1

Understanding computer procedures

Chapter 1   Programming overview.................................... 1
Chapter 2   Assembly language.. 14
Chapter 3   Programming in C#.. 27
Chapter 4   Compiler 40

Part 2

Programming paradigms

Chapter 5   Condition based procedures............................ 53
Chapter 6   Data structures 65
Chapter 7   Mathematical detail and analysis 76
Chapter 8   Functional based... 88
Chapter 9   Object orientated programming........................ 99
Chapter 10 Full Stack Programming................................. 108

Part 3

Creating applications

Chapter 11 Theory and appropriation design...................... 119
Chapter 12 Blinking LEDS in series.................................. 129
Chapter 13 Design of a simple program for a water station..... 139

FOREWORD

Without a concept of computer programming it is not possible to design a complex computerised system. This book aims to develop the understanding of computer procedures and how coding is created to achieve processes which many of today's modern systems used. By developing an understanding of how the computer interprets code it should be possible to improve the thought processes which underpin a typical program.

This is the final book of a compendium of three texts which offer the reader to understand the processes in computer and embedded systems design. The intention is that the reader is able to create their own strategies into creating and programming their own electronic systems.

PREFACE

This textbook is designed to allow the reader an understanding of how to program and adapt code to different types of systems. The perspective of the book is to highlight the structures and techniques which developers use to create their software. This s seen from a technical perspective as the book is illustrated with electrical concepts which underpin the functions which occur within embedded systems. Due to the concepts of the design of these systems being similar to other computerised processes it is possible provide an overview of how programs function, as well as some of the thought structures which create the logic for algorithms to work. Throughout the book coding practices are explained with the use of relevant examples which describe how the program functions and how the code is able to be written so that it is able to function inside a routine. The text should allow the reader the information necessary to understand how to program for themselves.

This text represents the final part of a trilogy of digital electrical books which explain to the reader how to design and program their own systems. The expectation of the trilogy of books is that the reader is able to create their own digital systems. The final part of the set is used to describe the processes which occur inside a computer algorithm when designing a piece of software.

PART 1

Understanding computer procedures

CHAPTER 1

Programming overview

In this chapter you will look at the following

- Software protocols and procedures
- How computers think
- Common computer systems
- Computer languages and data types

1.1.1 What is software programming?

Programming is the core assumption of computerised software. It creates the processes which allow the machine code to create procedures used within an application. For instance a small program might read the various inputs from a keypad and display the output onto an LCD. There might also be small subroutines which changes the output to the LCD by modifying the information to the I/O. An application like this has a number of considerations such as the type of embedded system used and what form of software is needed to complete the task. The interests of the text are to document and understand the types of procedures and languages which form the basis of software design. The focus of the book is to look at methods such as conditional and functional programming by using explanations written in assembler and C#, as they are the two most common forms of computer languages.

1.1.2 Why do we use programming structures and software?

Due to the complexity and possibilities within certain computer systems it is possible to develop code which can increase the number of tasks an embedded system is able to perform. For this reason programs are used as they are able to make the system more dynamic and versatile. For instance a small robotic machine which has a number of sensors which it uses to move around. It could be programmed in a number of ways so that it is able to better interact with its environment, depending on the hard written code. Here the program which is installed is able to be reconfigured and adapted to changes needed for the machine to conduct the various tasks. Due to the versatility of using a program it is better that certain systems are able to be reprogrammed and modified

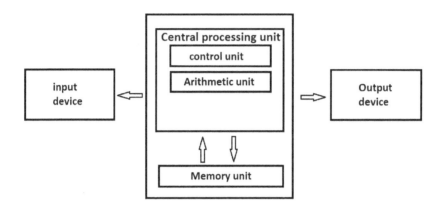

Fig: 1.1.2 Block diagram of a Von Neumann structure

Many types of embedded system merely use a CPU and memory attached to a number of I/O. In this way the device is able to commit a program to memory so that the outputs are able to be manipulated and changed. Many types of electronic systems are able to be improved through programmable adaptations and use this type of design. Being able to reprogram a device means that systems are able to use smaller amounts of circuitry and have wider adaptations. The versatility of programmable code means that many different types of devices are able to be reprogrammed, although the type of coding used, depends on the CPU and other relevant structures. Some types of designs are only able to provide a limited amount of calculations, meaning that some languages are not interchangeable and only specific to certain machines. For this reason coding is often specific to the device or intentions of the program. Writing effective code often means understanding the particular device.

TYPES OF PROGRAMMABLE SYSTEMS

COMPUTERS	I/OI devices
EMBEDDED SYSTEMS	Displays
ROBOTICS	Vehicles
GPS	

Table: 1.1.2 Types of programmable systems

1.1.3 Creating a program or procedure?

A program allows the computer to complete a task or function through the completion of a number of procedures which form the basis of the task. For instance if we ask the computer to create a calculation between two values, the computer has to carry out a number of steps or stages until the task is completed. This process is dependent on the device and the type of components, but the program would still have to step through the procedure in a number of stages. Each stage needs to be able to tell the computer the appropriate set of instructions to achieve the desired aim of the program. If we look at the program below it is possible to identify how this might be achieved.

Protocol 1:

```
Main
BTSFC BIT 8              //If byte set jump to sub
GOTO Subtract Subroutine
BTSFC BIT 7              //If byte set jump to sub
GOTO Add Subroutine


Add subroutine
Mov D, INPUTA           //Addition routine
ADD INPUTB, D
MOV D, ACC
```

```
Subtract Subroutine          //Subtraction routine
Mov D, INPUTA
SUB INPUTB, D
MOV D, ACC
```

Here the program moves between two sets of functions which performs the task of combining the two values. How this works is that depending on which function is selected the computer will choose the appropriate subroutine. Many programs are able to also follow this type of structure, in that a number of tasks can be written as routines which the computer calls during relevant points inside the program.

Due to the structure which exists inside a computer, there are a number of basic rules which dictate how a computer program is read by the machine. This means understanding the parameters in which a program is written. For instance computers read code line by line, and jump between points within the program's memory. For this reason a program needs to be able to accurately determine how the program is coordinated and contain separate parts for routines which the computer calls during runtime. There are in fact a number of rules needed for a computer to successfully interpret a program which can be considered the syntax or language in which the program is written. These mainly depend on concepts around structure. But also the rules which describe how functions are expected to work by the computer's memory and CPU. It is necessary to identify how a few of these concepts relate to the programming language.

1.2.1 Basic structures used within a program

As seen in the above program the code was written into a number of parts. The main part of the procedure coordinates the order in which the events occur. For instance the user has two choices which are called in turn which determine which subroutine is completed during the running of the file. This allows the program to clearly define the parameters which the user has to choose from and also determines the way in which the program develops. The main part of the program is responsible for creating the structure which the rest of the code adheres to, it allows each stage of the code to be run in turn. Meaning that it needs to be written in a coherent pattern that the program is able to follow. This is due to how a computer reads the code, the program counter needs to be able to return to the correct memory address, otherwise the instructions fail to be read correctly by the CPU.

Another element which relates to the topic of program structure is the call function or subroutine. This basically allows the program to commit to other functions which are stored separately from the main program. For instance a program might be written to calculate maximum numbers from a set or list. This could be written in the main part of the program. There might also be other processes which the program needs to complete such as working out the average of the set or finding the mean. These type of additions to the programs structure could be written as subroutines which are able to be added to the code and only called when the program designates, they are relevant to the running of the file. Subroutines basically push the current memory location onto the stack and allow the program to return to the main once they are completed. Allowing the program to conduct a secondary task or function.

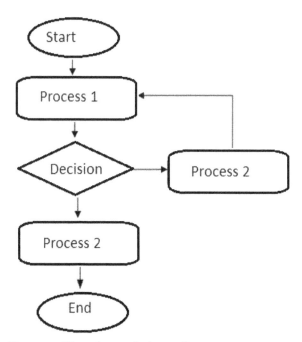

Fig 1.2.1 Flowchart of a basic function or process

1.2.2 Functions and protocols

A program often needs to run parameters and procedures which are used to perform calculations used by the program. For instance the routine below demonstrates a small function used to find the sum of two numbers using criteria to choose the type of procedure used.

Protocol 2

```
Main
If INPUTA < INPUTB          //Jump to sub
GOTO Subtract Subroutine
ELSE                        //Jump to sub
GOTO Add Subroutine

Add subroutine
Mov D, INPUTA               //Addition routine
ADD INPUTB, D
MOV D, ACC

Subtract Subroutine         //Subtraction routine
Mov D, INPUTA
SUB INPUTB, D
MOV D, ACC
```

Here there are two small subroutines which are used to either subtract or add the two values. These subroutines are able to create a function or procedure to perform the calculation. The program works by running this small procedure each time an event calls the parameter within the code. Functions are used a lot within programming, functional programming allows the developer to create parameters inside a routine by taking advantage of the CPU and the processor to manipulate values and data and also create small processes. For instance within the data analysis domain it is possible to use sort and retrieve functions which the program can use to find information contained within a data set. Here a function can be written which can be added within the code to store or search the information etc. Which improves the development of a program. For instance a large program might have a number of functions which ae used to add the depth to the functionality of the software.

Functional programming is an important topic area as it has its own rules and methods. There are a number of techniques which are able to be used within this from of coding which makes the program more adaptive and dynamic to change within a structure. This topic will actually be discussed in later chapters.

1.2.3 I/O and event handlers

Within an embedded application the I/O pins are able to process the signal sources which are sent from the sensors and switches to the ports. This provides the basis on which information and data can be read by the chip during a program. These types of events are able to transmit data and provide decision-based elements to the code. For instance an LCD might need to update information to the screen provided by the signal being input through a senor or a data relay. Effective programming uses these types of techniques to improve the sophistication of the program. Computers also use similar methods within a procedure. In that a program will often need to read the information from an input; or wait for a que provided from the I/O to complete the processes used within the program. For this reason it is import to understand how event handlers and interrupts are processed during a routine or protocol.

Within an assembly pattern the basis of an interrupt is to use something called polling which reads the status of the I/O register before loading the pattern which is being sent from the port. The assembly pattern uses a technique of calling the same pattern a number of times until a response is received for the I/O. To understand this process the below code is a brief example of a small polling procedure.

```
Watch
In A, STATUS
Bit 7, A              //Check status of interface
Jr Z, WATCH           //Jump to watch if not ready
```

Here this routine would be used to identify if a data set or input device is ready to submit information across the bus. This process is close to how the machine language might look, and describes the interrupt process within the I/O. This process is slightly different when using the C# language as certain process have their own calling functions. For instance, keypad and mouse presses have distinct procedures which are coded differently as they use separate processes for them to work. The C# language uses something called an event handler which is able to interrupt a program each time the event is called. For instance a small program to update the information on a list might need the user to provide a button click, which requires a separate event handler to record the input form the I/O, before committing to the procedure.

For instance

```
private void Button_Click()
{
    console.writeLine = "Button event interrupt")
}
```

Here the interrupt event allows the context of a label to become updated with the above text. As it is possible to identify the two languages use different forms of syntax or rules for them to work. This is due to how the languages themselves are interpreted by the compiler. Although they are used to achieve a similar outcome.

1.2.4 Memory maps and nested tables

Using the memory during the runtime of a program helps to reduce the duration of a programme and allows functions to be called without wasting processor time. For instance a program might use a nested table to lists a number of events by creating memory addresses for each of the procedures or call functions. For instance an LCD might have a number of retained memory addresses for the running of letters and numbers. This means that each time something needs to be called a simple memory address can be used to return the desired character. Using this same method could also be used to find functions and graphics which call data from required memory locations. It is possible to use nested tables for any of these reasons.

TABLE addwf PCL

```
retlw b'00111111' ;digit 0
retlw b'00000110' ;digit 1
retlw b'01011011' ;digit 2
retlw b'01001111' ;digit 3
retlw b'01100110' ;digit 4
retlw b'01101101' ;digit 5
retlw b'01111101' ;digit 6
retlw b'00000111' ;digit 7
retlw b'01111111' ;digit 8
retlw b'01101111' ;digit 9
```

Here the table above is used to count down a simple sequence using a list of numbers.

Memory locations can also be used to call variables, for instance the time and data of the current save might be stored as a variable within a memory address. Here the variable is updated by the program each time the save pattern is called. Here the program simply calls the routine and runs the current date time in the memory location.

Here

```
Public void timeofSave
{
DateTime = double
Var dateTime = dateTimeNew
}
```

By saving the variable in a memory location the data is able to be altered and changed. Rather than creating a constant element. This also means that during runtime, procedures which call the variable behave in different patterns each time the variable is called. For instance a criterion used to create a sequence of events might alter each time the procedure is called allowing for the progression of a dynamic algorithm or sequence of events. Making the program adaptive to events which occur during its runtime

1.3.1 How does the computer process certain procedures?

A program has to follow a set number of procedures or stages for it to be understood by the CPU and processors. This is one of the formalities of creating a program. Another important element to how the computer reads a program is through the syntax or use of expressions written inside the code. For instance an application might need to create a number of calculations during the running of a program and the entire process needs to be written as a series of statements or functions which detail how the calculation are expected to be created. The expression needs to be able to be understood by the program as the computer will only respond to the hard written machine code which is compiled in the data. These processes are important elements of how a program works and without understanding how the procedures are expected to read by the program the code has a limited chance of running through the compiler.

Being able to complete these types of processes depends on how the computer is actually designed. For instance many computers are able to complete a number of similar instructions. Although how this is achieved by the processor and the language might vary between machines, as the structure of the circuitry determines how the procedures are expected to be coordinated. The chips architecture determines intended application of the code.

1.3.2 How computers think

In many ways computers work quite differently to how we perceive and use number systems. A computer uses binary to convey information as data. This is very different to the decimal number systems which we use to create mathematical calculations and statistics. This is due to how the computer moves information, and also that the data is often used by different circuitry and paths. For this reason most types of circuitries are quite different to how they are expected to work. It is worth pointing out that understanding the devices circuitry is important to developing the code for the program. For instance the ALU found in the Zilog Z80 chip has only a limited number of commands. It is possible to create basic mathematical procedures using this chip, but is unable to carry out more complex tasks. It is simply not designed to complete this calculation.

For instance if a programmer wanted to work out the area of a circle. The calculation would need to be rewritten for the computer to understand the instruction.

Here

Area = 2pir^2 or
Area = 2 * 3.412*(2*R)

In fact the whole equation would have to be rewritten for the device so that each part is a single number and no brackets are used so that the computer is able to identify each value. This is due to how the computer interprets the information. In a computerised system the computer has no concept of priorities between different equations, and some formats are not recognised formulas. The computer in some way needs to contain the circuitry to understand the format. This is why asm formats are specific to different systems, and also why programming in C# needs a compiler to reinterpret the program into the correct machine code. For this reason it is important to identify the processes which the CPU is able to perform and also how the CPU is designed to complete the required functions and routines. A typical example of this is indexing in data structures. Modern computers have the circuitry prewired. Whereas older designs needed clear memory allocations to identify cell references. It was simply unable to perform the functions.

1.3.3 Creating a call procedure and the stack

The stack is used to store return addresses during call procedures and subroutines. It is also used to store local variables where they are able to be altered before they are removed, for example during the movement of data between registers. The stack is simply a small type of memory which saves information in a set way. For instance it uses the last in first out procedure. Which means that code needs to be written so that it identifies how to save the information and the call procedure during a routine. For instance during the running of a subroutine. The call address will be loaded into the memory first then any further variables or processes will then be added beyond this point. Before returning to the call address. This procedure is import to understand as it denotes the behaviour of the processor during the jumps between conditions and statements used by the program. The diagram below details how a program might use the stack between sequences.

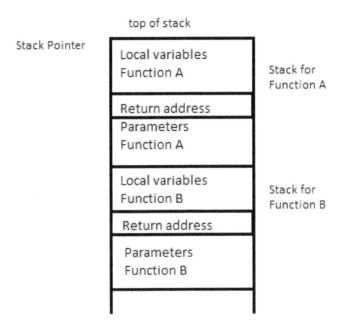

Fig 1.3.2 how the stack saves and retrieves parameters used by the PC

1.3.4 Floating point number and data structures

Due to the need to use complex number systems and data structures, computers are now designed to work with special types of commands. For instance binary systems find it difficult to multiply numbers which use a decimal point. This is due to the way in which the calculation is achieved by the CPU. For this reason many types of processors now have an adapted system which are used to work with numbers which have a decimal point. This new circuitry within the processor reduces the amount of processes needed to perform the calculation.

Indexing within data structures has also been improved by changing the design of the processor. This has been able to produce more accurate information and reduce the number of processes. Processors now use an AVX component which is able to create reference points in data tables, allowing multiple data references to be stored and manipulated by elements found in the program. For instance a list or table might contain varying data types, some of which need to be altered during a program into a different format. The AVX processor is able to instantly identify the relevant fields and alter the information found in the table. It also allows data to be searched and altered when called upon by the code.

Summary of chapter

The rest of the text follows a similar format in which types of software programming is identified and explained so that the reader is able to recognise the techniques and patterns used to create common processes and procedures. For instance data structures are identified and examined using examples in both assembler and C#. The purpose of text is to prove common software concepts using code which identifies the patterns used within software procedures. The expectation is that through explaining programming principles the reader has an explanation of how certain processes are created and coded.

End of Chapter Quiz

Draw a flow chart for the steps of a simple process?

Why is it import to understand computer structures?

List a few common compiler problems?

Identify two computer structures and procedures?

CHAPTER 2

Assembly language

In this chapter you will look at the following

- Types and uses of computer language
- Basics of assembler
- Examples of asm
- 16- and 64-bit programming

2.1.1 How do machines interpret code?

Computers work by interpreting the information received by the processor in the form of binary. Binary is a type of number system; in that it can easily be translated into a decimal format although the principle behind binary is slightly different. Binary is simply a number of 1's and 0's which represent a source of Vcc being sent across the bus during the runtime of a program. Computers store this form of information to create procedures read by the CPU during the running time of a program. For this reason it is possible to not only interpret binary as a number system but also a set of instructions in which a computers processor works. Being able to understand the instructions written in binary makes it easier to write the code needed to make complex computer processes.

Below is a simple 16 bit instruction written in binary. The first part of the instruction is the opcode, which designates the purpose of the code. The second part designates the information which is transmitted in the data.

Opcode	Operand
1111 0000	0000 1001

Here the instruction might refer to a function used in the ALU or accessing the I/O depending on the design of the machine. The second part of the code refers to a data byte or number. Depending on the type of system, an instruction is usually sent as two parts one for the instruction and the other for the data bytes. In this particular code the machine is telling the ALU to store the number nine in register B of the computers CPU. The computers CPU will have the necessary parts in the circuitry to send the data bytes into the relevant part of the memory. Due to the way the computer is designed. The binary found in an instruction will often be grouped or coded into processes which have similar types of purposes or systems.

The purpose of asm is to write code which is similar to the way in which a computer actually interprets information. For instance most asm formats write code in two distinct parts, which determine the instructions opcode as well as the data format. For instance a procedure might have a number of stages to move information across the registers and calculate the sum into the accumulator. The code might look like the following.

Mov A, 16
Add a, 8
Mov a, Acc

As can be seen from the code the first part of the instruction is the purpose or process, while the second command describes the data or value being sent. This forms the basis of writing in assembler and in many ways the language is the closest structure to writing in machine code, as it is possible to understand what the code might look like when written in binary. Another reason why this works, is that unlike C# the amount of code or lines which are written are identical to the amount of space which is used to store the information in the memory.

2.1.2 Grouping instructions

As already mentioned, instructions are grouped together by similar types of commands due to the way a CPU is able to process the information. For instance arithmetical types of commands might all be grouped within a binary reference. Meaning that the CPU is able to delegate these commands using the same form of networks, which reduces the circuitry needed to create the processor. This same technique would be used for all the different command structures, as to simplify the need for unnecessary components and networks. Below is an example of how a number of different instructions might be grouped under similar binary references.

0001 – 0100	Arithmetic
0101 – 0111	I/O processes
1000 – 1100	Movement between registers
1101 – 1111	Keyboard inputs

This form of instruction binding allows for the machine language to be easily interpreted and the code to be understandable to the developer. For this reason assembly is one of the easiest languages to interpret and reproduce within machine code.

2.2.1 Creating basic programs in assembler

Assembler is still a form of computer language in that its purpose is to use the machine code to create and run programs used within a system. Due to the simplicity of use, assembler functions best within small computerised systems. Which only have a small number of processes. This means that the coding for embedded systems or microcontrollers are quite uncomplicated whereas larger system might need a lot of work to achieve the same outcomes. For instance a small system might have only 64K of memory to download an instruction. Whereas todays computers would not be able to function with only this amount of RAM. It also means that some forms of coding in larger computers are more difficult than necessary, as each protocol needs to accurately create the correct instructions for it to work. Despite these flaws it is still important to understand assembler as not all instructions will function within C#. It might be necessary to hard write a process so that the computer is able to understand the procedure.

Within the asm language programs are able to still follow the same procedures of writing in routines, functions and processes. For instance a program might call a number of subroutines written under a number of parameters or criteria. The routines would be called upon when the program detects that a condition has been met. It is also possible to create procedures which form calculations and send and produce output to the sound and I/O by simply writing the code within asm. These programming techniques are still a requirement within asm, although some programming functions are out of scope for this form of language.

2.2.1 Creating a program procedure

As with most programs asm adheres to a logical a format to describe the structure and basis of the procedure. The language also require that all steps inside a routine are clearly definable and that the correct procedures are used for the movement of data between registers. Due to the way this is designed, some processes fail to function if the correct methods are not used inside the parameters. Meaning that the code needs to clearly follow a procedure without any parts missing inside the process. For instance the structure which was used earlier inside protocol 1 is a simple form for designing code. Here the routines are able to be called depending on the criteria and conditions specified throughout the program. The code is also able to accurately mimic the design of the CPU in that it adheres to the functionality of processes such as calculation and addressing.

The following example describes how to use the ports as an I/O. As can be seen the system does not need to use an interrupt or event handler as the ports are not used to que or parallel receive information. There is no protocol for the status register during I/O operations.

```
ANDI.B $SD              ; Select mode 0
BSET.7, PADA            ;Port A I/O mode
BSET.7, PADB            ;Port B I/O mode
MOVE.B, wreg            ;Configure port A bit 7 as output
MOVE.B, wreg            ;configure port B 6 and 7 as inputs

Main
MOVE.B,DREG             ;Input port B
ANDI.B #$0C0,D0         ;Retain bits 6 and 7
```

```
BTSCC
LEDON                              ;If both bits LOW, turn LED on
CMPI.B #$0C0,D0                    ;If both switches high, turn LEDon
LEDON
MOVE 0x00, wreg                    ;Turn LED off
JMP FINISH


LEDON
MOVE>B #$80,PADR                   ;Turn LED on


FINISH
JMP FINISH
```

Here it is possible to see that assembly follows a type of bit pattern where protocols and routines used within the program need to be clearly written so as to allow the protocols to jump between routines through the stages of the program

2.3.1 Basic instructions used in assembler

Assembler has its own format for writing functions, whereas C# uses declarations to create objects and classes within a program. Assembler creates a routine or procedure and under a parenthesis or return address. It completes these processes by grouping together a number of instructions until the entire process is able to create the function or procedure. A function is called a lot like an instruction and some instructions are actually a simple type of function. For instance the CALL function, needs to push the current memory location onto the stack before jumping to the routine requested by the program. The RETURN function completes a similar set of procedures, where the address provided on the stack is popped into the program and returns to the correct part of the program.

The table below clearly lists a number of types of functions which the assembler language is able to use within a program. For instance asm has a number of parameters for mathematical formulas as well as processes which are able to be used with string manipulation and output.

TYPES OF PROCESSES USED WITHIN ASSEMBLER

MATHS FUNCTIONS	Strings
CALL FUNCTIONS	Conditional statements
ADDRESSING	CSV's
FLOATING POINTS	

Table: 2.3.1 Functions used within assembler

2.3.2 Using addressing modes in assembly

Addressing is an important concept when writing code in assembler. This is due to the importance of writing literal values for each line of code. For instance moving bytes between registers can be achieved in a number of ways, although the circuitry used by the CPU is only able to work in a limited or set amount of ways. This needs to be considered when writing code as different computers use different conventions to establish addressing during command sequences. Addressing modes are simply the procedures used to move data between registers and components inside the CPU. For instance a simple command such as move contents between A and B can be achieved in a number of ways depending on the type of addressing used to move the data.

For instance consider the following lines of code in assembler it lists three types of addressing methods, for two types of commands

Mov B, 64	Literal value
Mov B, a	between registers
Mov B, 06h	from a memory location

Add B, a	Literal value
Add B, 64	between registers
Add B, o6h	from a memory location

Here the addition of two values can be achieved by the CPU under three different conditions, such as between register addresses, memory locations or a literal value. This explores a set number of ways in which the CPU is able to achieve a simple calculation process. These types of conditions within assembler are important as it denotes how the CPU is designed and configured to work. The assembler has to work in this way as it mimics the way in which the CPU is designed. The addressing methods merely explains how the circuitry is expected to work across the processor.

Different processors use different types of addressing practices. Such as direct relative and immediate addressing. These are the main forms of addressing, although there are a number of others as modern 64-bit machines are more complex and are designed to use more types of referencing of data between commands. As mentioned, it is an important concept within assembler as it designates the conventions used to develop code.

2.3.3 Using calculations in functions

Again the types of calculations used within a software program is dependent on the processor and type of machine being used. Most types of chips have an independent ALU within the processor which is used to perform the calculations. Meaning that it is possible to create an addition or subtraction protocol within many types of processors. Some processors are a little more complex in that it is possible to create loops and sequences using the shift and increment functions. Any type of calculation is dependent on the processor used and the possible instructions that are wired into the systems hardware. For instance the earlier chips were not able to process a decimal calculation which contained a floating point. Whereas modern computers include circuitry designed for this purpose.

TYPES OF PROCESSES USED WITHIN ASSEMBLER

ADD	Increment
SUBTRACT	Compare
MULTIPLY	Divide
SHIFT	Rotate

Table: 2.3.3 Basic arithmetical functions

It is now possible to identify a few sets of instructions to identify how the procedures in assembly work. Here are a few examples which use assembler to perform mathematical processes. These are not exhaustive but demonstrate how to manipulate bit patterns to create processes used within software.

Multiplying two values

```
Var MULT
XOR RDX, RDX          ; Clear registers
MOV RAX, 10
MOV RBX, 5
MUL RBX               ; Multiply contents of registers
MUL Var               ; Multiple var stored in memory
```

Here the response of the code is to create a value of 10 by multiplying 5 by 10. Then multiplying this value by the data stored in the memory location QWORD. Here the solution to the equation provides 100.

Here is another example using the increment function.

Incrementing a value

```
XOR RDX, RX
Mov RCX, 8F
Dec RCX
```

Again the code has a number of functions first the value in the register is incremented, as well as another process to decrement the value stored in the memory location.

The final function describes how to rotate the binary value stored in a register location.

Rotating a value

```
XOR RDX, RDX          ; Clear contents of registers
Mov CL, 65
```

```
Mov CX, 90
Rol CX, 8            ; rotate register 8 places
Rol CX, 8
SHR CX, 8            ; Shift register 8 bytes
```

This last piece of code describes how to rotate and shift the contents of a register. Again it is worth pointing out that these maths functions are basic interpretations of the ALU and are not complete processes used by the system. This level of programming is quite basic in that it would only be included as part of a larger process during a piece of software. For instance these types of commands would need to be repeated a number of times to produce statistics and data formatting within analysis software. In fact it would take many lines of code to create some of these types of processes.

2.3.4 Using strings and character data

The instructions which exist within assembler are able to handle strings and alphabetical characters in the same way that they handle numerical information. Although it is more difficult to manipulate the contents of a string, as it is only possible to compare the structure of two groups of characters. Variables are defined as a string within a program, as this designates the way in which it is possible to use the information which is presented in this form. For instance defining a value as a string tells the computer how to handle and decode the data. They are similar to numerical information in that it is a form of data which needs to be interpreted by an encoder before they are produced in other types of documents. For instance the information which is presented in a word document might originally be a form of stored data. Which is later decompressed and decoded by the system onto the new document.

The functions which exist in assembler for string data are quite basic in that they are used for storing and moving information contained in this form. It is also possible to scan information from other contexts before storing it onto the system. Again it is necessary to identify a few of the functions which assembler is able to provide for string data, to better understand the topic of using this form of data type.

Moving characters

```
MOV RDX 'FILESIZE'          ; size of file
CreateSTRINGarray           ; Create string array

XOR RDX, RDX                ; Clear registers
XOR R8, R8
XOR R9, R9
MOVE RSI 'FILESIZE'         ; Move source to destination reg
LEA RDI, dst
MOV RCX, SIZEOF

MOV DL, FILESIZE [0]
MOV R8B, FILESIZE [1]
MOV R9B, FILESIZE [2]
```

Here the source file has a list of three letters which are copied into the destination of three registers.

Storing contents

```
CreateSTRINGarray           ; Create string array

XOR RDX, RDX                ; Clear registers
XOR R8, R8
XOR R9, R9
MOV AL, 'A'                 ; Load A into registers

LEA RSI,                    ; Move source to destination reg

CLD
REP STOSB                   ; Store one byte at a time
```

```
MOV DL, dst [0]                    ; Load A into each register
MOV R8B, dst [1]
MOV R9B, dst [2]
```

As can be seen strings are determined by the size of the data in bytes. Information can be stored in bytes, words or double words depending on the length of the data. Storing and loading strings directly to a register depends on the byte size which exists on the processors CPU.

2.3.5 Calling parameters

Calling routines has already been mentioned in the text as it is important to the way in which routines and sequences are called during a program. For instance if a program needs to make a decision between two types of procedures or arguments. The call function is able to provide a jump event to load the memory address of the desired protocol. For instance there might be two functions which are stored in memory addresses 2400h and 3200h which designate whether the calculation is an addition or subtraction. The call parameter will load the memory address into the program counter and jump to this event when it is requested. The memory address does not appear on the program, instead the compiler designates where the memory address is located and each time the function appears in the code a call procedure occurs which pushes the memory location into the stack and program counter.

A similar event occurs with the return function as the original address of the program is pushed from the stack onto the program counter. For instance the program pushes both addresses onto the stack. The jump instruction is used first. The return instruction pushes the return address from the stack at the end of the procedure. This event takes place as the stack has a LIFO memory which allows information to be stored, and the compiler chooses the correct procedure for this to be popped onto the PC. This provides the function of jumping to the routine and returning to the program at the end of the procedure. There is a further explanation to the stack memory in chapter 1.

To illustrate how a program calls a return function the example below demonstrates how a routine might work inside a basic program

Main

LOAD R1, Count	; Load count into R1
MOV Acc,	; Clear accumulator
CALL MULT	; Call the subroutine MULT
LDR R2, MULT	; Load address of MULT to R3
STOP	

MULT

ADD R0, Acc, R1	; Add number into R0
SUB R1, R1, 0x01	; Decrement loop counter R1
BTSFC MULT	; Branch back if not done
PC ENDP	; Restore the address of PC ENDP
BCC, R0	; Local variable initialized
RETURN	

Here the program simply begins the procedure by passing the parameters needes for the protocol. This means that the registers are cleared ready for the calculation. The subroutine then loads the address of the SUM into register R3. Which creates the end of the instruction and the call procedure.

2.4.1 Summary of chapter

Assembler is the closest language to binary or machine code. This is due to the structure of the language closely resembling the instructional format of the compiler. For instance many instructions run straight from machine code in that the compiler does not need to create huge amounts of data to compile the code. The language is also simple to use in that subroutines and conditional jump statements are easily written in the program, using call procedures. Meaning that the structure is not overloaded with complicated terms. The chapter has aimed at providing a few examples into the terminology of code and instructions. With the intention of creating more complicated procedures later within the book. Understanding assembler is essential to perceiving how the computer interprets machine code.

End of Chapter Quiz

How is a program structure created in assembler?

Describe one advantage of programming in asm?

List why assembler is better suited to small processors?

Identify two computer functions used within assembly?

CHAPTER 3

Programming in C#

In this chapter you will look at the following

- Basic structures for C# programs
- Creating functions and event handlers
- Initialising objects
- Simple procedures in C#

What are the C+ and C# Languages?

These languages developed out of ordinary software coding such as basic and assembler, meaning that although these languages use different structures. The principles behind the two languages are actually quite similar. C# developed out of the earlier version of C+ and is slightly different as it contains the .NET references which has been modernised for programming contexts such as HTML and JAVA. The newer version is designed to work on the internet and includes protocols which are specifically for networking, communication and using the web. The .NET frame work has its own templates for designing applications which are able to be used across the web and console applications. Both versions contain a number of preinstalled functions which are used throughout a program to create the software definitions. The .Net framework allows for definitions within the library which are able to be called within applications that work across the net.

If we take a look at the following example, it is possible to better explain the concept of the systems library. For instance the following procedure is used to draw a circle from a list of shapes called my drawings.

```
static void Main()
    {
        circle = newDrawinCirc()
```

```
Shape[] myDrawings = newDrawinCirc()

foreach (Shape in myDrawings)
    Draw();
}

Console.write();
```

From the program it is possible to see that there are a number of functions which are used to create the circles graphical template. Functions are usually prefixed by two brackets, which means that this part of the code is a function or protocol. This particular protocol is able to draw a circle onto a new form or window loaded within the user browser. How this works is that the function is first written in assembler and loaded to a library. The user is then able to install certain procedures from the template library and use these within the program to create certain processes. This allows the code to contain procedures which are specific to certain processes or domains or are able to be used within specific contexts. The .Net framework is an example of a user library which is specific to web design and internet procedures.

Another form of functional library are the dll and CLS extensions which are often used within certain programming procedures when other extensions do not contain the correct coded pathways. C# contains the same procedural basis as the earlier versions which I will begin to explain in the rest of the chapter.

3.2.1 Creating a program structure in C#

In C# a basic program procedure Is similar to that found in assembly or other types of patterns. In that it needs to follow a certain set of parameters for the code to be coherent and also that the code is well written and able to progress within a clear pattern or process. If the program is not written within a clear set of rules the computer is unable to interpret the code, otherwise the program would stall or fail to work inside the compiler. For this reason the code has to be accurate and contain a valid structure which the computer can interpret. This means that the program includes a main procedure. The process used in C++ is a lot like the assembly language except some of the contexts are slightly different due to the conventions used by the compiler to interpret the events.

For instance C# has a number of ways of creating a subroutine, depending on whether the routine is expected to be used within a single parameter or within the entire document, as the compiler needs to be able to distinguish whether the return address is fixed or used again within other contexts. This is simply one of the ways in which the compiler makes sense of the code and is used to reduce the amount of dataspace needed to store the program. In fact there are a number of syntax issues which are used only within C#, although they are used quite logically throughout the program. This is due to the amount of instructions which the computer is able to use, although the basic structure for the program is quite simple when writing code in C# for computers which have a lower bit rate or structure.

3.2.2 Identifying basic C# structures

Within the C# language each procedure within the program is written within something termed a namespace. Each process which needs to be called within the program is written within its own memory reference, which the compiler is able to jump to or call when needed to within the program. For instance the program may have a set of procedures which exist within the main part of the program, and a few subroutines the program calls during certain events. Each event or procedure might have its own identifier which is used to create the memory location used when the program jumps to the routine. The identifier may also have a prefix which determines the functionality of the procedure. For instance static procedures are unable to contain variables which are altered. Whereas the public prefix means that the variables within the event are able to be accessed by each part of the program. The table below identifies a few of the programs parameters.

NAMESPACES AND PREFIXES	
MAIN	Static

SUBROUTINE	Public
FUNCTION	Private
TYPE	

Table: 3.2.2 typical namespaces used within C#

The code is divided into these parts so that the program is able to develop a structure and also to allow the developer to understand the contexts of each part of the code. For instance declaring a private void allows the code to contain information which cannot be altered by other elements of the program. This is important as the compiler needs to determine how to turn the program into machine code. The declaration of each element determines how the code is interpreted by the processor. It is important to clearly define each process as each element behaves differently within the program

Below is a basic program written with C. the program is written within an element called a main which is the start of the program and determines which processes occur first when running the routine.

```
Using System;
Namespace Calc

Static void Main()

Int X1;
Console.Write("Enter the Number");
X1 = Console.Readline());

If (X1 // 2 == 0)
Console.Write(X1 + " Number is even");
Else
Console.Write(X1 + " Number is Odd");
End
```

As can be seen the program merely determines if a number is odd or even and returns a print line on the console which states the type of input received. Here the program only contains one program parameter.

A second subroutine could be added which asks the user to add another value if the number which was input is odd.

For instance

Private void Subroutine
If (X1 // 2 == 0)
Console.Write(X1 + " you have chosen an even number");
Return

Here the program ends when the user inputs an even number. This example illustrates how a program can be separated into a number of procedures which it can call during different parts of the program.

As mentioned, the structure of the program is very important to the ability for the computer to interpret the program. It is also worth noting that a well written program can save memory space and create better processes and procedures. Which optimises how the program is coordinated within the computer's processor. It is now possible to determine a number of structures used within C and how they are used within the program.

3.2.3 Main, public and private voids

As we have seen the procedures used in the program are written in the main. Extensions to the program are written in the namespace declarations which are termed as either public or private. This is dependent on whether the definitions used within the extension are able to be used within the programs class or new definitions need to be created. For instance at the beginning of a program the variables used have to be defined to identify the method used by the compiler and decoder to interpret the information which is created in binary. A public void can be used when the definitions do not contradict other parts of the code. For instance if a procedure uses terms which are not included in the programs class, a private namespace is used to create a new object. Here using a private method or struct might mean specifying the definitions used in the procedure.

The following example describes two methods which are written in the same types of namespaces. For instance the definition below is a public procedure. The variables which exist in the procedure have already been defined in the class and are able to be used within the method. Here because the values have already been declared the function can be written as a public struct.

```
Namespace values
Public class
Int x = Input A
Int Y = Input b

Public int max (int x, int y,)
}
    If x>y
    Return y
    Else
    Return x
}
```

The second example is a private struct and declares the definitions of the variables. Here the private struct allows the program to control the content of the information within the routine.

```
Static void privateList
    {
    private int Collection;
    List<newEntry> list = new List<newEntry>()
    {
    new Candidate() {Entry = "Graham"},
    new Candidate() {Collection = 10, Entry = "Windows"
}
```

The final struct to mention is a void. This is a type of procedure which does not return a value. It is possible to use constants within a void, or for defining class operators. This would be when parameters are passed to designate call procedures.

3.2.4 Functions methods and subroutines

Routines are added to a program when the procedure needs to include other processes which occur after event handlers or certain conditions are met. A subroutine might also include a method or a function which is used to perform a calculation etc. A subroutine is simply another form of a struct and can be called at point in the program, but needs to declare whether how it is defining the variables within the procedure. As with assembler a subroutine is just another method of creating a structure to the pattern within the program.

Below is a simple subroutine which uses a true or false statement to identify for two values are integer.

```
Public bool returnNumeric()

Int X1;
If (int.TryParse(X1))
Return true;
Else
{
Return false;
```

3.2.5 Event handlers

Event handlers are often called interrupts as they are used by the CPU to interrupt other process during events within the I/O ports or status registers. Basically they are used to check the status of the port through a procedure called polling, which listens for certain events to occur in the program. Processes which occur in the I/O usually involve mouse clicks or keyboard presses, which are used to identify when a subroutine is expected to occur. For instance a program might be expected to produce a graph after it has performed a calculation. The subroutine will wait until the event handler identifies that a button has been pressed before creating the expected output. This event would trigger the subroutine to be called. Other event handlers include diagnostic processes and dialogue events.

The example below describes using a struct as an event handler to create a string output.

```
void interrupt button_Click()
{
    string Interrupt = "Start of Program"
    Consol.WriteLine = interrupt
}
```

3.3.1 Data types

We have already seen that namespaces are used to define objects and classes which exist within the programming space. The purpose of creating a namespace is to designate what types of values a property or an attribute will use when a procedure is called. For instance an application might have a number of inputs which are used within a calculation in the form of a numerical value. A procedure has to declare what type of value is being used so that the compiler is able to select from the correct type of procedure used for the particular data type. The process of declaring a set of values occurs within the namespace and is called the objects class. For instance.

```
Namespace Cars
Public class
String X = Make
String Y = Model

Public String getCars()
```

Here the declaration allows the compiler to identify the type of variable which is being used. This procedure is important to the concept of objects where multiple types of data are being used, which needs to be separated between different procedures. The declaration of variables is called within the programs class and this needs to be defined in each namespace or at the beginning of a private struct.

3.3.2 Creating variables and enumerators

Variables are important part of many procedures. They are used for calculations, as well as lists and tables. C+ offers a wide range of ways to manipulate and use data types. Another important consideration of data types is how they are stored and used during a procedure. The class of a variable merely describes how the object behaves and does not need to assign a value at this point. Assigning a context to a value allows the program to designate a part of memory to the variable. For instance

Var Modelboats = Ship

What this achieves is assigning a memory location for the string ship. This means that during a procedure the memory location is called and performs the string process within the procedure. It is possible to overwrite the memory location during a program for instance.

Ship = lifeboat

This is important during certain procedures where the program uses the data types to alter how the program responds. For instance a memory location could be used to pass a parameter to another procedure.

Another form of memory location for data types is enumerators or lists which save a number of values in a list where it is possible to jump between the locations within the list. For instance.

enum Months [January, February, March, April, May, June, July, August, September, October, December]

int main()

```
// printing the values of weekdays
For (Months [] January <= December++)

console.writeLine (Months)
```

3.3.3 Initialising an object

As we have seen with single variables and lists the data has to be allocated to a location in memory. This allows the procedure to call the reference as prompted throughout the program. Without this process the memory would be deleted each time it is called. This same process happens with objects. An object is a group of values which often do not share the same data type. For example a list might contain the following.

Var Cars = string
Var model = double
Var OwnsOne = Bool
Year of model = Integer

Initialising an object or class or data type means allocating a new location in memory to the procedure. Initialising a construct usually means creating a new instance of the object. For example

Carstype Type1 = carsType new

Or

Carstype Type 2 = CarsType new

This would create two instances of the object cars type. Which would create an object which contains a number of values as designated by the objects class. This allows the program to understand the location of the data and the type of information stored.

3.4.1 Properties and attributes

A property can be used within a program to specify a particular instance within an object. For instance the model within car type is an instance a property within the object. Attributes are used in a similar way. In that they provide and extension to the class terms of the value. For instance it is possible to serialise an objects value alphabetically by turning the strings values into order. The attribute creates a method of using the particular type of data from the class.

3.5.1 Creating procedures in C#

C# has a wider range of procedures than assembler. The C# language has rewritten certain process so that a single command can be used to create a process. For instance it was seen that in assembler it is possible to create a loop by decrementing the program counter and jumping back to the original part of the routine for instance.

MULITPLY

Add b, 64
Add a, b
Dec b
JNZ b
Call Multiply

C# has its own set of procedures to create the same loop procedures. For example a For Loop will create an iteration of a process each time it is called.

```
Int number = 20;
console.writeLine(" Please Enter any integer");
console.scanf(number)

for(i=1; i<= number; i++)

   total = total + i;

console.writeLine(Sum of natural numbers is: " + total);
```

A while loop creates a similar procedure except the loop stops each time a condition is met. For instance a program might repeat a process until the counter runs to zero and the process stops. Below is an example of a while loop.

```
int number;

console.readLine("Please Enter a value below 10 ")
console.scanf(number)

while (number <= 10)

    total = total+number;
    number++;

console.writeLine("the while loop ran", + total);
```

Procedures will be covered In more detail in later chapters. The last main procedure to understand here is the else if function. This is used to determine if a condition is met before moving onto the next procedure. These types of procedure formats are important to the concept of conditional programming as it is used to achieve the direction or flow of a program. The code below is an example of a else if statement within a program

```
int marks;
    console.writeLine ("Enter you subject Marks:\n");
    console.scanf(marks)

if(marks >= 50)
    console.writeLine ("Congratulations")
    console.writeLine ("You have passed")

else
    console.writeLine ("You Failed")
    console.writeLine ("Better Luck Next Time")
```

Summary of chapter

The chapter has covered some of the important concepts within the C# language. Due to the complexity which exists within modern computers it is no longer possible to commit to long procedures written in assembly. C# is able to provide the same functionality as assembler for a larger dataset. The chapter has tried to overcome some of the concepts which underpin the C# language and provide examples of how the structure and programming is achieved. This is not exhaustive of the entire language but hopefully some of the important processes have been discussed. It is important to note that C# is a type of language which is often not accurate in terms of how a procedure should be designed as the compiler is responsible for creating the machine code needed for the programs.

End of Chapter Quiz

How is an event handler used within a program?

Describe how a function is relevant to a program?

How are variables defined within C#

List a set of procedures?

CHAPTER 4

Compiler

In this chapter you will look at the following

- How a compiler works
- Different compiler programs including MPLAB
- Lexical and syntax issues
- Decision trees

4.1.1 What are the functions of a compiler?

Compilers are an important concept to software programming as they turn the written software program into the binary machine code used by the processor, during a program. Compilers have a number of functions depending on which system it is being designed for. For instance it is likely that a compiler will include a debugger as well as some form of simulator which can test the program while it is being written. It is important to point out that compilers work differently depending on the system or the language the code is written in. Usually there is a form of design wizard which is able to determine how the system is expected to function. For instance some types of chips in embedded design have different pin outs and register coordinates. Meaning that the machine code is different depending on the chip which is being written onto.

The software wizard is able to determine how instructions are formatted within particular chips or system, and provide the correct machine code for each particular instruction. Meaning that the design of the assembler language is the same between chips and does not need to be rewritten or formatted onto a different design. The aim of the chapter is to determine the uses of a compiler and provide examples into their purposes and how the compiler is able to interpret the code. The topic of computer compilation is able to better describe how the software is making decisions and creating the processes. Without an understanding of the compiler it makes it difficult to create programming structures which the system will understand. For instance formatting inside the compiler is extremely important to writing a piece of software which will work inside the machine.

4.1.2 Different types of systems

There are mainly two types of systems used for compiler software. There are those which are for embedded systems which use assembly language such as MPLAB. There are also compilers used for computer systems which use a C# compiler such as visual studio. This chapter intends to explore both systems for the two separate designs. As they both use similar principles to format chips and create programmable software. The first system MPLAB is primarily designed to format microcontrollers. These are chips which have a separate RAM space for loading a procedure and are integrated into chips which have their own ALU and processors. Embedded system are slightly less complicated in that they are usually designed around 8 bytes of data drive and have a limited instruction base. Most embedded systems have fewer than 256 instruction types, which are limited to simple calculations and movements between registers. MPLAB offers the best compiler to program these chips.

The compiler used within MPLAB offers a programming space which uses assembly code to create the instructions. This space allows a program to be written and debugged before it is formatted to the chip. The code is written within the compiler and formatted to the specific instructions used within particular chips. The wizard creates the format for the instructions. Which are specific to the intended chip. Due to the fact some chips have a larger set of instructions than others this is important in that the formatting of the chip is relevant to the intended design. Despite this principle most microcontrollers use a similar format of instructions between chips.

TYPES OF COMPILER PROCESSES

FORMAT INSTRAUCTIONS	Simulate programs
CREATE SOFTWARE	Create binary files
DEBUG	Format chips
FORMAT LIBRARIES	

Table: 1.1.2 Functions of a compiler

4.2.1 Using the MPLAB IDE

The picture below shows how the IDE inside the software works. There is a window space for the programming of code. This includes the assembler format for each instruction, which can load and save files needed to create the program for the chips. The IDE also contains a number of separate windows which can provide a viewing space for registers and port I/O procedures during the running of a program during simulation. The IDE is adapted to use a number of devices and can directly load the binary files from the IDE to the chips. Navigating the compiler is quite simple in that it is possible to view a number of document windows for any single program.

Fig 4.2.2 the MPLAB IDE

4.2.2 Debugging software and simulation

Although it is possible to create a program on the compiler the main purpose for the IDE is to debug and compile the code ready for formatting to the chip. The compiler works in assembler by taking each instruction and formatting this into the relevant data bytes in binary. For instance

Mov a, b
Add 64, a

These instructions would be written in two lines of 16 bytes and be converted by the compiler into the following code.

1110 1100 0001 0001
1110 1101 0100 0000

This is what the chips processor would use to convert the data into an instruction. Each instruction written in the assembler is converted into machine code for the specific chip sets. This is done during the compiler process. The entire document for the program is checked into the correct machine code. During this process the compiler is also able to debug the program to determine whether the program is written accurately enough to work within the specific chip set. This means determining if the instructions are written correctly and if a procedure is able to be completed by the chip. A common debugging problem is not using the correct format for an instruction. Or procedures failing to work when stepping through a particular stage of the program. The debugger is able to correct syntax and provide a list of errors for the program.

Once the compilation of the program is complete and error free the program is then able to be simulated by the Ide and the processes checked, this is to determine how the ports and registers are programmed to respond during each procedure. For instance a program might need an input from a specific pin on each port before jumping to the next program. Here the simulator is able to provide a window for the ports or registers, which identify the existing byte reference during each procedure. This is achieved by a separate window which provides an input stimulus to update the information contained in the watch windows.

4.2.3 Software programming in Visual Studio

Visual Studio exists a lot like MPLAB in that it is able to create the program for a piece of software as well as simulate and debug the written code. Again the IDE uses a series of windows to control the content of the program and provide tools which are used to turn the program in effective machine code. Unlike assembler, Visual Studio does not need to differentiate between different types of chip structure. As the code on most 64-bit machines contain the same set of instruction architecture. For this reason the code written in Visual Studio should be directly compatible with the device it is being designed on. Although Visual Studio can be used within a number of ways. The main purpose of Visual Studio is to compile and debug the programs written on the software, into effective machine code and applications. It is worth noting that because of the extended set of instructions found in 64-bit machines, C# is slightly more complicated than other forms of language.

Below is screenshot of the Ide and windows used within Visual Studio. It details the windows and tools which a developer can use to code and design a program written in C#

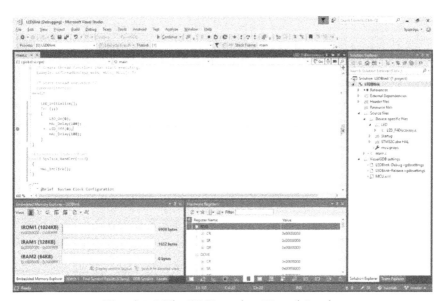

IFig 4.2.3 The IDE used in Visual Studio

44

4.3.1 How does a Compiler create the correct machine code?

It is now possible to describe how a compiler is able to convert the program from the C# into meaningful machine code. This process occurs in a number of stages which analyse parts of the code and return the instructions as binary. To achieve this the code needs to be broken down and transformed into a number of tokens which are used to identify each process within the program. These tokens or chunks of information are passed through parameters to interpret if the codes syntax ad structure are able to create an actual pattern within the machine code. The whole procedure occurs in a number of stages, which tests the logical arguments found within the code. The diagram below describes the stages in the procedure.

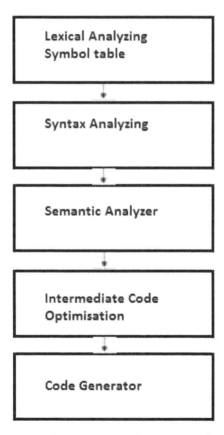

Fig 4.3.1 stages within a compiler

4.3.2 Lexical analysis of code

The first process which occurs within the compiler is something called lexical analysis. This is the term used to take each part of the program and create a token using something called a symbol table. What this does is determine the type of instruction which has been written within the code. For instance, if the code is a string value, operator or type of function. This process is used for a number of reasons as it allows the logical statements which exist within the processor to be checked against the syntax used within the code. By breaking the code into parts the compiler is able to check if logical conditions which exist in programming structure, are relevant to the types of conditions called within the program. The below table describes the tokens used within the compiler. During compilation the tokens replace the code to check the syntax.

Symbol table

Identifier	Var	Number	0,34
Keyword	Else, if	Quote	""
Separator	(), &	Bool	True, False
Operator	+, -	Data Type	Integer, string bool
String	"Hello world"		

Table 4.3.2 symbol table used within the compiler

Here the entire document will be cross referenced against the table, which allows the compiler to determine whether the code contains appropriate types of language, and also checks if there are mistakes and unnecessary terms used by the program. This is part of the debugging process of the compiler. This is separate to turning the code to binary. It merely allows the compiler a way of determining if certain conditions are met. As the compiler then has to perform a number of processes to optimise the code and select the correct procedures between processes. Which means the compiler needs to first reinterpret the code into a meaningful form.

4.3.3 Understanding syntax analysis

This is the most important procedure completed by the compiler. As the logical structures within the program are checked against the logic arguments needed to perform each type of instruction. During this stage of the compiler the software checks the program for errors contained in the structure, the arguments used and the types of parameters used by functions when declaring variables. For instance the structure of the program is checked by determining that each of the routines call and return instructions work in the correct way and the program does stall when calling new routines. This is important as the program needs to return the correct part of memory during each instance of the program's dialogues.

A further process completed by the complier is to identify how objects and variables are parsed between parts of the code during the use of the values instance. Here the compiler needs to determine that the correct procedure is used to decode the value which is being used within the procedure. For example the protocol below is used to declare that the variable Score will be used within the code namespace as an integer.

Dim Score As int

This means that each time the variable score is used within the program the variable needs to be parsed against the correct structure in the computer for the program to work. Here the compiler checks each instance of the object to determine the correct types of procedures are used when calling this variable. If the compiler identifies that the code does not use the correct syntax the debugger would signal that an error has been produced by the code. During compilation the debugger will create an error list for each instance of non-functioning code.

4.3.4 Using logic trees to verify arguments

A syntax tree merely takes the tokens and determines whether the arguments contained in the program are able to construct the relevant procedures needed for the code to run adequately. Here the compiler takes each argument in turn and returns a value if the conditions are met during each stage of the procedure. For instance the argument above for the variable declaration is checked to determine if the code is written within the correct syntax.

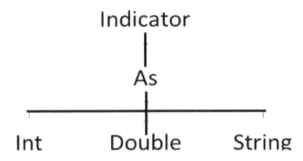

Fig 4.3.4 A basic syntax tree

Here the argument would be referenced against the syntax tree. Which describe the parameters needed to pass the particular argument. It is possible to see that the indicator is followed by the relevant set of tokens which means that the statement used to declare the variable is recognised by the systems analyser inside the compiler.

Logic trees allow the compiler to understand the conditions which need to be met for each argument within the code. The compiler takes each token in turn a cross references each type of procedure against those found in the logic trees. This is one of the methods in which the compiler is able to debug the code for errors, and check the logic for the relevant statements. This needs to be passed before committing the program to machine code. As the debugger is able to note any errors in the program and create a log of the definitions needed for the program to be created.

4.4.1 Intermediate code and optimisation

Once the code has passed the syntax and semantic evaluation the generator is able to produce a set of binary machine code, which reflects the instructions used within the program. The code at this point is merely an example of working code used by the compiler to test the functionality. It is then rewritten to optimise the code. What happens here, is that the compiler determines how to reduce the amount of data needed to write the binary, taking out parts of the procedure which repeat routines and method statements. The compiler uses a set of assumptions which identify repetitions within the program and unnecessary terms used within functions and routines. The compiler at this point is able to use this technique to reduce the amount of lines needed within the code and optimise the size of the data for better performance.

At this point the code is also checked against the methods used within the functions to call procedures. This is important to the allocation of registers and parameter passing. For instance variables declared throughout the program are expected to be read and used by the correct type of register or data type process. Meaning that the compiler evaluates the procedures chosen to pass datatypes through the processor. Another important part of this procedure is to allocate memory locations to objects and variables which initialises the memory location and parsing procedures. For instance during a call and return function. The compiler needs to decide how the memory addresses are saved onto the stack during the procedure and return the correct point in the program when the instructions return form the routine.

The compiler decides upon these processes during this stage of the program. Allowing the program to commit to the correct procedures used by the processor.

Summary of chapter

In this chapter we have been able to look at the types of compilers used by different systems as well as the functions and purposes of compiler software. Due to the various procedures which it takes to analysis a program before creating the machine code. Compilers need to be able to perform complex tasks such as syntax and semantic analysis. This makes the interpretation of machine code difficult to perform without the compiler. The role of the compiler is to complete this process and provide a list of errors without having to achieve this manually.

End of Chapter Quiz

List how compliers are different between languages?

Determine potential coding errors within a program?

Describe the Lexical stage of the compiler?

Describe register allocation during optimisation?

PART 2
Programming paradigms

CHAPTER 5

Condition based procedures

In this chapter you will look at the following

- Programming domains and paradigms
- Decision based programming
- Creating a programming flowchart
- Conditional programming procedures

5.1.1 How do we use different programming domains?

Due to the range and the types of software which are available a number of different contexts have evolved around different types of programming. The concept of creating different software practices falls under the heading of domain theory, which is essentially creating a group of rules and procedures which are used within a particular domain or platform. For instance within data structures the type of software which is created needs to constantly use functions and procedures which sort, retrieve and catalogue information. For instance a common procedure within data structures is to retrieve information stored within a group of indexes. This allows the program to find information when requested by the user. By ascertaining the type of domain a piece of software is aimed at. It is possible to develop a set of coding practices which are better suited to the design of the program.

DIFFERENT TYPES OF SOFTWARE DOMAIN	
CONDITION BASED	Control systems
DATA STRUCTURE	Mathematical
ROBOTIC	Function based
NETWORKING	Object orientated

Table: 5.1.1 Basic arithmetical functions

For instance networking procedures need to store information which is available between locations. There are also conventions in which this type of data is handled and the format in which it is displayed. These kind of concepts separates the platform form others meaning that the code which is developed should ideally be specific to the type of domain it is being used within. For this reason it is necessary to create a number of conventions or practices which underpin the types of coding which are used within separate domains. This makes code more appropriate between applications and more relevant to the software it is being designed for. The purpose of recognising domain theory is to develop software programs which are a better design for the intended purpose. The topics contained in the second part of this text refer to understanding the principles behind different domains and their applications.

The importance of understanding domain theory is due to the contexts which exists between different types of procedures. Code has to be accurately developed so that it is able to function within the system it is designed for. For instance using techniques which are better suited to a design allow more versatility within code.

5.2.1 Decision based programming

Decision based programming is common to many types of software format. In that a program is expected to change or perform routines, due to the events which take place during the program. For instance a small robotic vehicle might need to make decisions for the direction of travel according to the inputs received from a number of sensors. Here the vehicle might respond to sensors which determine whether to turn the vehicle once it gets to an obstacle. The program needs to respond to the sensor by turning the vehicle so that it can avoid the obstacle, creating a new condition or response to the event. This concept of condition-based responses underpins the concept of the theory. In that it is possible to create meaningful programs and procedures based on the occurrence of events which occur within the program.

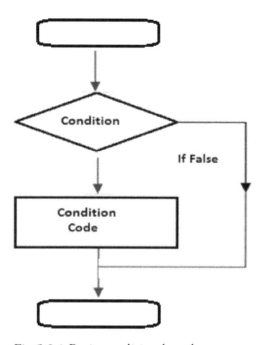

Fig 5.2.1 Basic condition-based program

As already mentioned, domain theory is used within a number of applications, such as automation or data analytic software tools. The concept of condition-based programming is important to understand as many types of programming can be improved through applying decision-based assumptions to the software.

The idea of condition-based programming relies on the concept of reacting to criteria or inputs to change the current output of the program. In fact it is possible to use a range of parameters in which to base a decision. Such as electrical sensors, criteria changes or event handlers which are responses from peripherals attached to the computer. The program below describes a decision-based program which ascertains school grades based on the mark achieved within the final year.

```
int main()

    float Score;
    char grade
```

```
console.printLine("Enter marks: ")
scanf(Score)

grade = marks >= 90 ? 'A' :
    marks >= 80 && marks < 90 ? 'B' :
    marks >= 70 && marks < 80 ? 'C' :
    marks >= 60 && marks < 70 ? 'D' :
    marks >= 50 && marks < 50 ? 'E' : 'F';

console.printLine ("Your grade is ", + grade)
```

Here it is possible to see that the output for the final grade is based on the decision of results for the end of year. This is a form of criteria-based decision process. Although it is also possible to use stimulus responses and automated processes to create similar events within a program. This is simply determined by the type of process and program being used. The concept is still relevant whether making statistical assumptions or mechanical movements

5.3.1 Using graphical tools to create programs

There are a number of techniques which can be used to visualise how a program is expected to respond throughout the course of the procedure. For instance if a program is expected to perform a number of events under different conditions. It is useful to display this information as a flowchart first before writing the code; as it allows the programmer to visualise the events and create a set of routines based on the behaviour of the programme. The routines could be anything from movements, to performing statistical procedures depending on the status of the program. The flow chart allows all the events within the programme to be displayed within the one graphical tool for a better understanding of the entire procedure. To better explain this idea, below are two examples of flowcharts which describe the processes within a program.

Example 1

The program is a piece of software which monitors the processes on a control system for a grid. It needs to create two types of reports depending on whether the system is working smoothly or inaccurately during a specific timing schedule within the year.

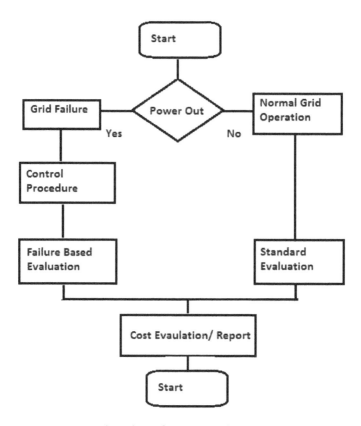

Fig 5.3.1 Flowchart for a control system monitor

From the diagram it is possible to see that the program has to catalogue the information which is received under a number of different headings before creating a report which lists the recordings of outputs from the control system. The flowchart allows the programming to visualise the structure of the program and how the routines are expected to be coordinated throughout the program.

Example 2

This second example takes the information which is presented from a group of questionnaires and determines the type of statistical assumptions to use within the software package.

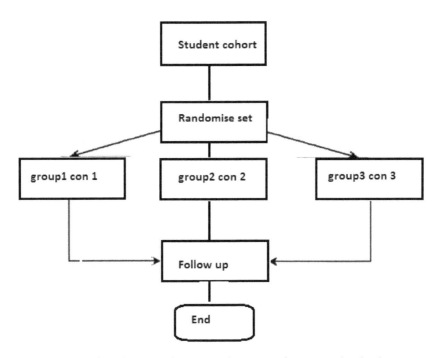

Fig 5.3.1 Flowchart to designate the type of statistical calculation

Again the flowchart is able to describe each step within the process and create a branch or series of events which occur after this event. The flow chart is able to better understand how the decisions within the program are expected to occur.

5.4.1 Creating condition-based procedures

The events which happen within a program rely on some kind of change within the parameters of a condition or input for the program to change its sequence. Effectively the program needs to be effected by some form of change in event for a condition to be met and the program to proceed to the next protocol or memory reference. The chapter has already mentioned a number of ways in which a program basis a decision within the examples in the last section. It is now possible to describe the procedures which are used to create basic decision formats and some examples of the programming language needed to create this effect. Below is a table of typical decision-based procedure statements.

CONDITION BASED STATEMEMTS	
JUMP WHEN ZERO	True, false
IF, ELSE	Compare
GREATER THAN	Event handler
EQUAL TO	

Table: 5.4.1 Basic arithmetical functions

5.4.2 Using event handlers

Within C# there are a number of event handlers which it is possible to use within the contexts of a program. The most common form of event handler is a simple button click event meaning that a button has been clicked within an application. For instance a small program might use a button to calculate a number of values which have added to the input boxes of a label. Here clicking the button within the application create the process of adding the values together to create a sum of the total. This process creates an interrupt within the pattern of the program and would commit to running the procedure used to create a sum of the values. Other event handlers include, dialogue boxes which record errors and also handlers which create an interrupt sequence at the change or end of an event.

Below is the code which might be used to write the program procedure to display the result of the input button being pressed? Effectively what occurs is that a call subroutine starting at its own memory location is called when the user operates the event handler. This event creates the process of interrupting the program and starting the routine.

```
    private void Button_Click()
    {
Input = inputNew
    int sum = 0;
    int x = LablleBox1
    int y = Lablebox2

Console.writeLine (x+y)
    if (int.TryParse(Double)
    {
    sum += result;
    console.writeLine()
```

Event handlers are useful in many types of procedures where the program needs to respond to a peripheral from the I/O or any type of event which uses interrupt handler or listeners which wait to respond to external procedures. Event handler basically create the process of waiting for an event to occur by polling the current status of a register.

5.4.3 Using If, else and case switch

These two types of statements form the basis of most kind of procedures needed to program a decision event within a routine. The If statement is possibly the most common of the two. What occurs here is that a condition is tested and creates a number of events depending on which statement occurs to be true. This is useful when a process needs to test the truth of an event before the program proceeds. If the statement is false the program can deter and create a secondary process.

For instance the program below states a simple command which counts the number of characters in a password which either creates a command prompt or moves onto the next program.

```
if (x > 10)
console.writeLine = ("Input exceeds the amount of characters")
else
InputDialouge()
```

This procedure can create one of either two events. It is also possible to add further possible statements using the elseif statement as below.

```
if (x > 10)
  console.writeLine = ("Input exceeds the amount of characters")
elseif (x<5)
  console.writeLine = ("Input does not contain enough characters")
else
  InputDialouge()
```

Here the extra condition allows a further process to be added to the procedure allowing the program to create more functions form the one protocol.

The next type of statement is the case switch statement. This is used when there are multiple types of output where there is no difference in priority or likelihood of any of the statements occurring. Instead the first condition which occurs is the trigger to the next event procedure. The protocol for the case switch statement can be written as the following.

```
switch (someChar)

case 'a': RunPartA;;
case 'x': RunPartB;;
case 'y':RunPartC:;
case 'z': RunPart:;;

default: actionOnNoMatch;
```

Here the return address of the protocol is the case statement which the program jumps to. The protocol begins by declaring that it is a switch statement which needs to designate the criteria used to create the input stimulus.

5.5.1 Creating a criteria-based decision

Event handler's deal with something called interrupts which mainly work with information perceived form the I/O. This is not the only way of using condition-based programmes as it is also possible to use criteria's which base decisions on the comparison of two values. Although the logic behind these two processes are similar in that they simply jump to a new location within memory, when a condition has been met. Criteria based sequences mainly use values as the basis of a decision and merely determines if a type of statement is true or false before determining the behaviour of the program.

The example at the beginning of the chapter used a set of criteria to work out the flow chart for a chain of events. The program was used to create the basis for a statistical procedure to ascertain the numbers of student candidates at the beginning of a year. The entire program used criteria matching to evaluate the truth of a number of events. Criteria matching works by using the compare function within the ALU to effect the status register. Here a single byte is produced in the status register if an event is true within the compare function. A program can check the status of the register and coordinate the program based on this event. Criteria matching is a simple form of creating condition programming and can be used in many ways.

Consider the following program it creates a procedure which uses two inputs and evaluates which value is greater before moving to the next part of the sequence. Here the compare function is used to work out if a carry flag is set when the two values are processed within the ALU. This procedure allows the program to determine which event occurs next within the sequence.

The flowchart for the procedure might look like the following.

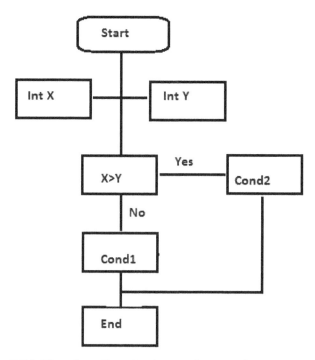

Fig 5.5.1 Flowchart for criteria matching within a program

Here the code could be written with C# as the following. Also instead of a write line the code could jump to a new part of a procedure. Although the conditions for writing the program would be able to remain within the same format.

```
int time = Input a
if (time < 18)

    console.writeLine ("Good day.");

else
    console.writeLine ("Good evening.");
```

The code used here uses a compare function to create the decision as seen in the flow chart. Within the C# language there are a number of types of programming tools which can create similar conditions within the status register to determine the outcome of events. For instance a greater than compare function can be used as well as Boolean values which determine if a condition is true or false. The Boolean value can be used in a number of ways to compare two values.

For instance

```
int x = 10;
int y = 9;

If x>y = True
FunctionA()
Else
FunctionB()
Return
```

Summary of chapter

This chapter has looked at how domain theory can be used to create better and more relevant programming procedures between different types of platforms. Condition based programming is one type of domain platform used mainly within data tools and automated processes. Using decision procedures within an application allows the program to coordinate events from other stimuli and inputs. Making the program dynamic and reacting to outside events. Although this can be considered its own form of programming technique. It is possible to use condition-based procedures in many types of application,

End of Chapter Quiz

Describe how types of domains differ between platforms?

Name a number of ways to decision processes?

Draw a decision tree or program flowchart?

Create a program which uses a number of condition-based procedures?

CHAPTER 6

Data structures

In this chapter you will look at the following

- How programs use data structures, such as SQL
- Data capturing, storage, statistics demographics
- Techniques such as indexing and memory allocation
- Procedures used in data structures

6.1.1 Using data structures as its own domain

As we have seen in the last chapter, a platform can be considered a domain when it uses its own set of specific tools and techniques. Software often uses the same types of coding and rules to determine data structures, for this reason this form of programming can be considered to have its own domain. The concept of programming behind data structures is to create a way of storing information so that it can be easily accessed and modified as needed. For instance information which has been grouped together into certain forms of data types might need occasional modification and updating periodically. Meaning that there needs to be a set of procedures which can easily access and modify the information, without altering the quality of the data. The purpose of understanding data structures Is to create appropriate ways and techniques of storing and manipulating the data.

Data structures are used in many types of programming such as statistics, demographics as well as internet applications for commercial industries. Making the concept of data applications important to a wide range of topic areas and potential software designs. In fact there are so many ways data can be stored and analysed that it is possible to conceive a number of potential practical uses for this type of software programming. The table below lists a range of topics data structures cover within software engineering.

PRACTICAL USES OF DATA STRUCTURE TECHNIQUES

DEMOGRAPHICS	Statistics
DATA ANALYSIS	Data Visualisation
STORAGE AND CAPTURING	Data manipulation
DATA ORGANISATION	

Table: 6.1.1 uses of data storage techniques

There are a number of ways in which a program might need to store a group of data. This could be for the purpose of referencing information, storing data bases. Or creating a list or table of information which can then be used within another application such as a graph. There are many formal types of software which use data structures such as excel and access. Whereas there are some forms of data applications which are used to store large files sizes such as SQL. Which is able to gather information and use the database within other applications.

6.1.2 Ways of using information as data

Data capturing is the process of taking information found from any type of source and converting the information so that the data present within the resource can stored and modified within a computerised format. For instance a company might often create a report on figures and information such as sales, profits and losses. The information which is gathered for the report can also be stored within a number of different data types, so that the information can be modified and manipulated into more meaningful sets. This could be in the form of a graph or demographics which bring more detail and structure to the information. The purpose of capturing data is to not only store the information. But also modify and use the figures or values in a more descriptive way.

Once the information has been converted to a computer format. It is possible to use ways of cataloguing the information such as by data and time. Information can also be stored within reference materials such as grouping information by category or reference. This process allows the data to be manipulated and stored for reference or conversion at a later date.

Many types of industries use this method of cataloguing information due to the need to store and retrieve reports which are an important basis for decision processes etc.

6.1.3 Algorithms, demographics and statistical reports

Making use of data is not a new concept as there are many types of processes which can be used to find information from just a basic report. The role of computers within this topic has been to automate the procedures, so that creating and analysing data can be done on a simple process which is achieved through computerised software. For instance it is possible to create a number of types of algorithms which use a mathematical procedure to gather information from within the data. For instance an algorithm could be used to work out the average sales of a product, or understand which part of the year was considered the peak time for sales. This kind of information is obviously useful to the company, a computerised system is easily able to take the data and perform the calculations to improve the quality of information gathered.

The program below finds the sum and average of a set of numbers. The user inputs the numbers and a value is given to designate the average value for the set.

```
public static void Main()
    {
    int x1, x2, x3, x4, x5, avg, sum;
    console.writeLine("Enter 5 Numbers:");
    Scanf(x1)
    Scanf(x2)
    Scanf(x3)
    Scanf(x4)
    Scanf(x5)
    sum = (x1 + x2 + x3 + x4 + x5);
    avg = (sum / 5);
    console.writeLine("Sum :" + sum);
    console.writeLine("Average :" + avg);
```

The code above is one type of simple algorithm which can be used on a set of data. In fact there are many ways in which algorithms can be used. Here the program simply takes the information presented in the data or group of values and reinterprets the information through the use of mathematical procedures. This could mean preforming a process of converting the information to a graph, or taking parts of the data to write a report on information which has been gathered between certain timeframes within the year. In fact there exist a number of possibilities in which to allow better interpretation of data by simply using a computer process or algorithm

Using the data to create demographics and statistics, means using algorithms which are able to convert and manipulate the data. Statistics resides mainly on information such as means and averages, which uses formulas to recalculate the data.

For instance a program could be used to understand the standard deviation of a group of values.

```
public static double StandardDeviation
    values = List[8, 9, 5, 4, 6]

    return values

public static double StandardDeviation

    double mean = values.Mean(start, end);
    double variance = values.Variance(mean, start, end);
    return Math.Sqrt(variance);
```

Here the algorithm is used to create a statistical assumption from a table of information. Demographics work in a similar way. The data is captured or gathered and through the use of algorithms it is possible to provide visual tools such as graphs to display the results of statistical detail or analysis. For instance algorithms can be used within a graph to interpret correlations, mean and max values as well as regression lines. It is possible to create the procedures within a program or software to provide these types of reports within the analysis of the data. These types of software patterns allow for the meaningful reinterpretation of data used within a company or entity.

DIFFERENT TYPES OF SOFTWARE ALGORYTHMS	
CORRELATIONS	Standard deviation
REGRESSION LINES	Variance
MEAN, MAX	Compound interest
CLUSTER GRAPHS	Differentiation of a vector

Table: 6.1.3 Mathematical procedures used with programming

6.2.1 CSV's and how computers store information

Storing data involves a number of programming methods which are used to create spaces and folders which identify the location of the data within the memory. Essentially each part or section of data is stored within a memory location. For instance a data sheet might contain a number of references which are used to separate the data into different cells. Each section contains a separate chunk of data. A program is able to identify each file in a number of ways. The most popular way of creating a data table is to use a method called indexing which creates a space within the folder and jumps between locations by using a reference point to jump to different memory indexes. It is also possible to use hash tagging of memory types, as well trees and lists which are able to create the index of the different cell reference. We will now look at each in turn.

6.2.2 Using an index to store data types.

This method is the most straight forward although it often uses more amounts of data to create the structure of the data table. The principle behind indexing is working out how memory data cells are needed for the table and the size needed for each data cell. For instance a table might appear as the following.

Car index table

Make	Model	Year	No. doors
Toyota	Micra	1974	3
Nissan	Premier	1968	5
FIat	Townie	1971	4

The table displayed here describes a dataset containing in a matrix of 3 x 4 meaning there are 12 cell indexes for the table. What the program might do to store this information is create 12 location each with 64 bytes which is enough memory to hold the information of an entire cell. How indexing works is creating a initial cell reference to jump between points. For instance if the programmer wanted to find out the year of the make of the Nissan car. The program would jump to 8 memory locations of 64 past the initial marker. The computer completes these types of procedure each time a cell of row is called. The computer would simply retrieve the information.

For example, here is a typical set of data.

Int Array [10] (1,3,2,5,4,7,6,9,8,10)

This is one way of storing data as a simple table or list. Many computers use a similar method of creating a data space for a table and using the memory references between points. Form here it is possible to search, retrieve and insert new information to the table. The computer uses something called CSV which is able to work out the specific memory reference for each part of a data structure or table.

6.2.3 Hash tagging

This method is similar in that each item is stored within a specific order in memory. But instead of a memory location each cell is given a reference number or hash code, which the computer uses to retrieve information. Although the principle of the two formats is quite similar. A programmer would have to use separate types of programming procedure, to shift the reference cells through the processor to retrieve the required information. This method can be used in a number of ways, and is perhaps better suited to small data sets which contain variations in size of information.

Indexes used in a Hash table

Index Ref	Value1	Value 2
0	Nissan	Premier
1	Fiat	Townie
2	Toyota	Micra

As can be seen from the table each cell reference has index which the program can search through when retrieving information.

Within the program the search function might appear as the following.

```
struct DataItem *search(int key) {
 //get the hash
 int hashIndex = hashCode(key);

 //move in array until an empty
 while(hashArray[hashIndex] != NULL) {

  if(hashArray[hashIndex]->key == key)
   return hashArray[hashIndex];

  //go to next cell
  ++hashIndex;

  //wrap around the table
  hashIndex %= SIZE;
```

6.2.4 Linked list or trees

Linked lists are used for information that is grouped together such as a column or cell row. How this works is that each data set is stored with a link to the next cell reference at the end of the list. In this way the program is able to coordinate where in memory the contents of the table are stored. This type of indexing causes a number of difficulties when retrieving information from large datasets. As the programs has to be able to locate the memory address of the current cell, before moving onto the other parts of the program. For this reason it is better suited to large data types than date sets.

Another form of this type of coding is a linked tree. Which again uses a reference at the end of the data set which identifies other types of cells which are linked to the initial reference.

The overall problem which exists with linked lists and trees is the modification of information and creating new data sets within the table. The problem being that altering the reference within one set of data can mean having to change the entire list. Which is a lot more difficult from a programming perspective.

6.3.1 Procedures used within data structures

Due to the contexts of using data structures it is necessary to use code which is specific to this type of programming practice. For instance code needs to specify what types of procedure it is using to search or alter a list. Data tables are able to use different methods to store and index the information which is being used. It is also important to note that data structures are considered a separate domain within programming and have a number of procedures which are specific to the structure used to store the data. The compiler is actually responsible for this part of the coding but this is a consideration of writing code for these types of processes in C#. Below are a few types of procedure which are used for common processes such as searching retrieving and editing information. The way in which this is achieved depends on the form of indexing which is used such as referencing or linked lists.

6.3.2 Using two forms of sort within a data table

Sort is such a common function within a data table that it is possible to use a number of programming techniques to create a sort process. The main two forms of sorting a list or group of values is achieved by creating a procedure for a merge or bubble sort function. Merge sort works by splitting the values into two and creating a new list one item at a time putting the values back into list in order. The bubble sort archives the same function except that the final value is achieved by taking the second value and placing it before or after the first value. Below is an explanation in C# for both types of function. It important to note that with a data table sorting the list often means altering every value.

Here is a bubble sort function

BubbleSort(list)

```
  for all elements of list
    if list[i] > list[i+1]
      swap(list[i], list[i+1])

end
```

Here is the same function using a merge sort

merge(var a as array, var b as array)

```
  var c as array
  while (a and b have elements)
    if (a[0] > b[0])
      add b[0] to the end of c
      remove b[0] from b
    else
      add a[0] to the end of c
      remove a[0] from a
    end if
  end while

  while (a has elements)
    add a[0] to the end of c
    remove a[0] from a
  end while
```

```
while (b has elements)
  add b[0] to the end of c
  remove b[0] from b
end while
```

6.3.3 Other functions used with data structures

Another procedure used for capturing data in sets is an insert method which adds a new value to the data table once it has been created. Here the place within the table needs to be specified for the place of the new value.

```
// Function to insert x in List at #location
insertNewEntry(int n, int List[],
    int x, int location

//change position in array
  for (i = n; i >= #location; i--)
    List[i] = List[i - 1];

  // insert x at #location
  List[#location - 1] = x;

  return List;
```

The final procedure to mention is deleting a value within a data set. Here again the location within the table is identified and the value removed from the list.

```
int main()

  int List[#5]
  console.printLine("Enter 5 elements")
  for(int i=0;i<5;i++)

    scanf(List[i])
```

```
console.writeLine("Enter index to be deleted")
Scanf(n)
List[n] = null
```

Summary of chapter

The purpose of this chapter has been to identify how data types are stored and accessed within a computer's memory. Due to the wide range of applications which exist for data manipulation and demographics. Data capturing is an important topic within computer processes. As it is possible to automate many forms of calculations which industries are able to use for the purpose of reports and end of year statements. To identify the area of data analysis the text has tried to highlight some of the techniques and procedures which are used within these processes. This s only to highlight how an application might be designed for data at a basic level of understanding.

End of Chapter Quiz

Identify a number of purposes of data capturing?

Describe the role of statistical data demographical tools?

Design a procedure to create a report for monthly earnings?

How might a CSV be designed within assembler language?

CHAPTER 7

Mathematical detail and analysis

In this chapter you will look at the following

- Basic formulas and syntax
- Graphs, statistics and data analysis
- Algebra
- Advanced formulas

7.1.1 Using data structures as its own domain

Mathematical processes are relevant to a range of applications and do not need to be used within just the one type of context or design. Math type functions are able to be used within many types of procedures and the context of this chapter is to understand exactly what a processor is capable of achieving in term of interpreting formulas and performing calculations. Instead of focusing on one type of platform or process. The chapter will look at a number of types of mathematical statements which explore how the CPU within a computerised system, can be used to determine the answer to calculus and equations.

7.1.2 Determine if a number is odd or even

To get started with the concepts of mathematical equations. It is necessary to understand how the ALU inside a computer is able to process information. The processor itself contains a module called the ALU which is used to manipulate information received in binary. Very small processors such as those found in microcontrollers, have a limited range of mathematical procedures. Usually there are only able to add subtract and decrement a group of registers. More modern computers have a wider range of instructions meaning that the ALU is able to create a larger group of calculations or functions. Meaning that the instruction set is able to perform the calculation without committing to a complex procedure.

As many mathematical expressions use a range of functions. Procedures which the computer is unable to do, can be completed by carefully performing a procedure which is able to provide the desired response. The equation below is a typical type of computerised procedure which is able to ascertain if a value is odd or even. How this works is that the number is divided by two. If the result is even a Boolean expression is used to identify the vale as true

```
class Program
    static void Main()

    int i;
    Console.Write("Enter a Number : ");
    i = (Console.ReadLine());
    if (i % 2 == 0)

        Console.Write("Entered Number is an Even Number");
        Console.Write("Try another number");

    else
        Console.Write("Entered Number is an Odd Number");
```

It can be seen from the equation that the computer is unable to assume that the value is odd. What the processor achieves is dividing the number by two and checking the status register for a binary response to determine if the sum has left a remainder. Essentially the program checks the status register to determine the expression. Many types of procedures within a computerised system work within a similar way in that a process needs to be completed which is in the form of a number of different procedures.

Understanding the logic of a system is important when creating or designing a procedure. Another consideration within mathematical process is the syntax used to describe basic algebra. Fortunately C# does not struggle with problems of basic syntax although, it is worth pointing out that some software types cannot ascertain where the start or beginning of an expression occurs due to the way in which formulas are given priorities within algebraic expressions.

7.1.2 Creating basic expressions for the sum and the product

As mentioned, the processor used for the C# language is able to perform basic algebraic conditions such as creating a sum or product of two basic values. This type of procedure can be added to any kind of function allowing the processor to determine a multiplication or subtraction etc. for any set of given values. The program below allows the computer to create a type of calculator within a console application, to determine the sum of two values.

```
class Program
   static void Main()

      int input1, input2, result;
      char Choice;
      Console.Write("Please enter the first of two numbers : ");
      Num1 = (Console.ReadLine();
      Console.Write("Enter the Second Number : ");
      Num2 = (Console.ReadLine());
      Console.WriteLine("Main Menu");
      Console.WriteLine("1. Addition");
      Console.WriteLine("2. Subtraction");
      Console.WriteLine("3. Multiplication");
      Console.WriteLine("4. Division");
      Console.Write("Please decide on the option for the calculation");
      option = (Console.ReadLine());
      switch (option)

      case '1':
         result = input1 + input2;
         Console.WriteLine("The Addition of the two values obtains: {0}",
         result);
         break;
```

```
  case '2':
    result = input1 - input2;
    Console.WriteLine("The Subtraction of the two values obtains: {0}",
    result);
    break;
  case '3':
    result = input1 * input2;
    Console.WriteLine("The Multiplication of the two values obtains:
    {0}", result);
    break;
  case '4':
    result = input / input2;
    Console.WriteLine("The Division of the two values obtains {0}",
    result);
    break;
    default:
    Console.WriteLine("Invalid Option");
    break;
```

As can be seen the program is able to interpret basic algebraic expressions to create the console app. The program merely determines a set of rules which allow the instructions to be read by the compiler, before being rewritten into machine code. These types of decision processes are decided by the structure of the hardware. For instance most arithmetic units have a basic level of binary manipulation. Where as more sophisticated computers are able to use more complex mathematical structures.

7.1.3 Using exponents

Exponents are a common maths problem as they are used to solve equations which aim to find the area or radius of a given surface. An exponent is essentially a value which is used to create a multiple of itself. Exponents are usually described as square values or the power of a value. Below is a procedure to find the answer of an exponent to a value. This is completed in C# using the Math pow condition which is able to create a calculation to provide the answer.

```
class Program
   static void Main()
      Console.WriteLine("Enter the Base : ");
      float num = (Console.ReadLine());
      Console.WriteLine("Enter the First Exponent :");
      float exp1 = double.Parse(Console.ReadLine();
      float mul;
      mul = exp1;
      Console.WriteLine("Result is : {0}^{1} : {2}", num, mul, Math.
      Pow(num, mul));
```

As ca be seen here although the processor does not contain the ability for the ALU to complete this expression. The library found within the C# namespace (Math) is able to create the necessary asm format inside the compiler. Essentially the compiler module runs a procedure which creates the equivalent response.

7.2.1 Mean and standard deviation

Mathematical principles such as mean and standard deviation are used primarily within statistical analysis of data tables and lists. They allow for information to be assessed for how the values obtained within the data are relevant to other forms of related research. Statistical validation of information allows for data to be comparable and substantiated within other forms of data.

The programs below identify how a procedure can be created using statistical functions. Again it is worth noting that most procedures are only relevant to the compiler and the processes already identified in the program. The basis to start a procedure is by creating the data to be used within the list.

Here is a program to work out the mean of a set of values.

```
class Creating a mean
public static void Main()
```

```
int n1, n2, n3, n4, n5, avg, sum;
Console.WriteLine("Enter 5 Numbers:");
Input1 = Console.ReadLine();
Input2 = Console.ReadLine();
Input3 = Console.ReadLine();
Input4 = Console.ReadLine();
Input5 = Console.ReadLine();
sum = (input1 + injput2 + input3 + input4 + input5);
avg = (sum / 5);
Console.WriteLine("Sum :" + sum);
```

Here the program is able to use a function called average which is able to create the procedure to work out the average of the sums.

The program below is used to create the procedure for calculating the standard deviation of a set of numbers. This is the amount of variation which occurs from the average or mean. It would also be possible to use a formula and create the same expression using a calculation procedure.

```
public static double StandardDeviation()
    {
      return values.Count == values.StandardDeviation
    }
    public static double StandardDeviation()
)
    {
      double mean = values.Mean();
      double variance = values.Variance();
      return Math.Sqrt();
```

7.2.2 Bar charts and regression lines

It is possible to visualise information which is captured as data by creating graphs and charts which are able to portray the information in a visualized form. The purpose of creating a graph is that it is more visually striking and able to convey more meaning than figures alone. The two programs below describe making a graph in C# and creating a regression line from the information.

Below shows a procedure for creating a bar chart in C#

```
public void BarExample()

    chartControl.Series.Clear();
    // Data arrays
    string[] Animals = {"Cat", "Dog", "Bird", "Monkey"};
    int[] Points = {2, 1, 7, 5};
    // Set palette
    chartControl.Palette = ChartColorPalette.Balanced;

    // Set title
    chartControl.Titles.Add("Animals");
    // Add series.
    for (int i = 0; i < Points.Length; i++)

        Series Graph = chartControl.Series.Add(Animals[i]);
        series.Points.Add(Points[i]);
```

Linear regression lines are used to show the average values within a data set. For instance if a report is split between the times of the year. A regression line can be used to display the averages which exist between these points. Again the program below describes how this can be achieved in C#.

```
private static LinearRegression()
    {
    var Y = new DoubleVector();
    var Min = MinAverage();
    var Max = MaxAverage();

LinReg= new LinearRegression();
Plot XY ()

    return linReg;
```

7.3.1 Creating procedures for mathematical problems

C# has a wide range of mathematical terms which are able to be added directly to a function in the same way it is possible to use the value for a sum or product. The computer uses the compiler to create these processes, but during a program the terms can be added interchangeably using the abstractions used within algebra. For example it is possible to use the cos of a value by simply adding this definition to the function. Below are a number of console applications which use a variety of methods for the user to specify the terms within the formulas and create an output which is dependent on the type of expression used.

The first program is an expression used to find the acceleration of an object given the value of two inputs such as time and velocity. The program is simply a calculation which divides the speed of the vehicle by time. This algebraic expression is actually quite simple as it uses a set of standard processes which the computer can easily carry out.

```
The acceleration of an object
    static void Main()

        int velocity, time, acceleration;
        Console.WriteLine("Enter the Velocity: ");
        velocity = Console.ReadLine();
        Console.WriteLine("Enter the Time: ");
        time = Console.ReadLine();
        acceleration = velocity / time;
        Console.WriteLine("Acceleration at " velocity " is : {0}", acceleration);
```

The second program works out the volume of a spherical object by calculating the surface area and performing another procedure to work out the volume. This simply uses a number of terms to complete a series of linear equations.

```
The volume of a sphere
public static void Main()
        double radius, surface_area, volume;
        double PI = 3.14;
```

```
Console.WriteLine("Enter the Radius: ");
radius = Console.ReadLine();
surface_area = 4* PI * r * r;
volume = (1.25) * PI * r * r * r;
Console.WriteLine("the surface area of the object is : {0} ", surface_
area);
Console.WriteLine("Volume of Sphere is : {0}", volume);
```

The next equation is similar to the first in that the formula is to understand how many miles have been covered by inputting the speed of travel and also the time taken in hours. The equation is again a formula to interpret the mathematical expression used to designate distance through velocity

Distance speed and time
public static void Main()

```
    int speed, distance, time;
    Console.WriteLine("Enter the Speed(km/hr) : ");
    speed = Console.ReadLine();
    Console.WriteLine("Enter the Time(hrs) : ");
    time = Console.ReadLine();
    distance = speed * time;
    Console.WriteLine("Distance Travelled (kms) : " + distance);
```

This last expression finds the cosine of a value for the use within trigonometric functions. The purpose of the equation is to work out the cosine of a given value within the formula cos(x) where x is the value to be multiplied.

Find the cosine of a value
static void Main()

```
        x = Console.ReadLine()
        Console.WriteLine("Calculated cosine of " cos();
```

```
static double cos(x)
    double p = x * x;
    double q = p * p;
    return 1.0 - p / 2 + q / 24 - p * q / 720 + q * q / 40320
    - p * q * q / 3628800;
```

7.4.1 Creating functions in class libraries using asm

Occasionally a code might need to be hard written, which applies to any type of domain programming. Here the library used within the application might not be able to commit to a routine or have the necessary function list to complete a process. This would mean that the code or routine would have to be hard written in assembler or machine language for the computer to understand the procedure. Here instead of using a function form the system library, the code would be written in assembler and pasted into the program.

Below is a program which uses an example of how asm is used to create a program. There are two functions used here for multiplication and division. The expectation is that the reader will understand how to create an asm procedure for their own code, if need when creating a new function or process.

```
Multiply two numbers
_start:

mov ax, 5 ; // input1 = 5
mov cx, 10 ; // input2 = 10

mul cx ; //Sum = ax *cx

    mov    AG,1      ;file descriptor
    mov    AG,4      ;system call number
    int    0x80      ;call kernel
    mov    CD,res
    mov    CD, 1
```

```
mov    CD,1      ;file descriptor
mov    AG,4      ;call number
int    0x80      ;call kernel
mov    AG,1      ;call number
int    0x80      ;call kernel
```

return

To illustrate the concept further here is a second procedure to divide tow numbers within asm. The program could then be copied to the relevant folder within C#.

Division of two integers
mov ax, 5 ; // input1 = 5
mov cx, 10 ; // input2 = 10

div cx ; //Sum = ax *cx

```
mov    AG,1      ;file descriptor
mov    AG,4      ;call number
int    0x80      ;call kernel
mov    CD,res
mov    CD, 1
mov    CD,1      ;file descriptor
mov    AG,4      ;call number
int    0x80      ;call kernel
mov    AG,1      ;call number
int    0x80      ;call kernel
```

return

Summary of chapter

Mathematical procedures form their own basis of coding practices in that the code can be generated and used within many different types of applications. The purpose is to generate a procedure which the computer can understand and be used within abstract formulas and then integrated into a programme. The chapter has explored how the compiler interprets mathematical instructions and also how it is possible to create independent code which can be added to its own directory or library. C# offers many mathematical functions which can be used within procedures. Not only is it possible to create algebraic expressions for mathematical procedures. The compiler is also able to create graphical details and regression lines. Where it is possible to use these techniques in demographics and statistics.

End of Chapter Quiz

Explain why some compilers interpret algebra in different ways?

Create a function to find the area of a circle?

Why might some code need to be hard written?

Explain how an assembler program is used to create a difficult algebraic expression?

CHAPTER 8

Functional based

In this chapter you will look at the following

- Concept of functional programming
- Applying functional programming
- Examples of code by context
- Differences to object orientated

8.1.1 How does functional programming work?

Functional programming is designed around the basis that during a program the application will have to complete a set of procedures which evaluate a group of values or data sets. This means that a method or function is created which perform this procedure. Within any type of programming it is possible to use a function to complete a statement. Functional programming basis the entire protocol for writing the programme within the concept of functional procedures. This is achieved in a number of ways which define this form of programming within its own context to other types. Themes which underpin this style include modularisation and mapping and the format for declaring variables. This means that setting data types occur within the function rather than the namespace. Another important point to consider within the domain is return values, as statements create a new product or entity within a struct.

8.1.2 Evaluating a functional based procedure

To explain how the terms work within the domain of functional programming, it is necessary to look at a simple procedure for working out the area of two types of shapes. C# has a number of ways in which it is possible to create the inputs necessary to perform this calculation. For instance object orientated programming declares a set of data types within the class which the rest of the procedure can use within a namespace. This allows the compiler to retrieve the correct instruction type dependant on the types of variables used. The complier works in a similar way within functional programming except it is possible to declare values while writing the function or at the beginning of the procedure. The reason for this is that the arguments which form the procedure are usually written in the brackets which designate the terms.

The compiler returns the statements written by the function and also cross references the data types and procedures written as part of the function. This process is completed at a different time within the compiler. The example below demonstrates this concept of abstract properties. The programme below takes the lengths from the sides of a circle or square and returns the output as a string statements.

Example of a program to demonstrate abstract properties.

```
using System;

public abstract class Shape
    private string myEntity;

    public Shape(Shape)
        entity = shape;

    public string entity
        get
        return myId;

    set
        myId = value

public abstract double Area
    get;
public override string ToString()
{
    return type + " Area = " + Area);
public class Square : Shape
```

```csharp
    private int mySide;

    public Square(int side, string entity)
      : base(entity)
      mySide = side;

    public override double Area
      get

        // Given the side, return the area of a square:
        return mySide * mySide;
public class Circle : Shape
    private int myRadius;

    public Circle(int radius, string id)
      : base(id)

      myRadius = radius;
    public override double Area

      get
      // Given the radius, return the area of a circle:
      return myRadius * myRadius * System.Math.PI;
```

As can be seen the declarations used within the procedure occur within the brackets of the function. Here the argument square contains the two data types which are used by the procedure to form the calculations and write the result. This is also seen in the second equation for the value of the radius and the string answer. Effectively this has been written twice for each equation, although object orientated programming would have declared the values at the beginning of the statement.

This forms one of the main contexts of programming within the functional domain. Another principle of the style is that procedures can also be written within the brackets of an argument which are able to perform a number of events in series. This procedure is used to declare the functions as well as items which exist in the statement argument. This is used when a number of procedures are written within the entire document and the items are intended to be used interchangeably.

8.1.3 Using transparent values

Due to the concept needing to use datatypes for variables and return values. Data types are written within the context of transparency. The data types are declared with their own namespace meaning that the contexts of a formula or procedure are unable to be altered or interfered through other contexts. This means that multiple items can be written within a programme as constant value which does not affect the working of other patterns. Consider the following statement

Area of a circle

Rda1 * 2pi
Circle Rda1 = New circle rad

Here it can that the argument has its own memory space for creating the input values for the argument. This means that the argument can be used interchangeably throughout a number of procedures without affecting the information contained in the original variable or argument. This forms the basis for argument statements. Writing in this way allows statements to be used interchangeably, and that the argument will not alter the information contained within the variable and effect other procedures.

8.1.5 Writing a statement in function based

Due to the way variables are declared and the parameters which form the basis of functional programming in the compiler. This form of programming also effects the way statements are written within the programme. The language uses its own form of creating arguments which can be seen within the method statements. The following two statements are used to perform the same function within the two types of styles.

Functional programming example to create an object.

```
Function createPerson(Firstname)
Const obj =

Obj.name = name;
Obj.greeting = function
Alert('Hi I am ' + this.Firstname + ',');

Return obj

Let newperson = createPerson('Jeff')
```

Here is the same procedure for creating an object except this time the programme is written in object orientated programming. Which uses a different set of rules to create the pattern.

```
Function Person (name)
This.Firstname = name;
This.greeting = function
Alert(' Hi! I am ' + this.Firstname + '.');
```

Which uses a slightly smaller number of procedures within the compiler.

8.2.1 Examples of procedures for different datasets

Having explained some of the differences which exist in function based programming it is possible to explore some examples of creating procedures using this format. This is mainly to identify how processes are created for typical types of method statements. The chapter has already mentioned that due to the differences in dataset types, the format for fuctions often varies between variables and types of procedures. For instance creating do while loop within a search function has its own method statement based on the purpose and declaration and values. The examples below details some of the typical structures which exist within a functional programme.

8.2.2 Creating a GOTO function within a struct

This can be used to create a loop within a process to complete the procedure again until an outcome is achieved within the protocol. This is an example of a basic procedure which is common to many types of program.

```
// goto function

class Program
    static void Main()
    int number, per, option;
    float answer;
loop:
    Console.Write("Enter a Number :");
    number = Console.ReadLine();
    Console.Write("Enter Percentage Value :");
    per = Console.ReadLine();
    answer = (float)(no * per) / 100;
    Console.WriteLine("Percentage Value is:", answer);
    Console.Write("Calculate again press 1. To quit press digit:");
    option = Console.ReadLine();
    if (option == 1)

        goto loop;
```

8.2.3 Null able values

Nullable values are a type of variable declaration which can also contain no value. For instance a data cell can contain any type of integer value, but also a parameter for containing no value at all. This is important when declaring specific context to types of variables. One of the uses of this type of declaration, is creating an exception handler or parameter, which a procedure can call if the variable has no information. For instance a pattern may repeat itself and stop when the variables memory location has a null value. Which is similar to using a Boolean condition within a procedure. The below example is for creating a function using a nullable variable.

```
// Nullable values is where the data set does not need to contain a value

namespace Application
    class Nullables
    static void Main()

    int input1 = null;
    int input2 = 10050
    double input3 = new double();
    double input4 = 3.14157;
    bool boolinput = new booinputl();
    Console.WriteLine("Nullables : {0}, {1}, {2}, {3}",
            Input1, input2, input3, input4);
    Console.WriteLine("A Nullable boolean value", boolinputl);
    Console.ReadLine();
```

8.2.4 Tuples and object declaration

Tuples are essentially variable declarations. But is necessary to develop the concept of how this works within a program. Basically an object is created which contains a number values, each with its own data type. Items within the object are then able to be used throughout the procedure. The below example shows how to declare an object.

```
//These are used to express data sets.

Random rnd = new Random();

Tuple<double, double> RandomPoint() {
    var x = rnd.Double() * 10;
    var y = rnd.Double() * 10;
    return Tuple.Create(x, y);
```

8.2.5 Brackets

Again this procedure has already been mentioned within the chapter but explains how to declare variables within the definition of the function. For instance a function might contain a number of data types which need to be identified during the method statement. For this reason the variables are defined within the brackets of the procedure.

```
// Declaring the datatypes within the procedure

static double Distance(double x, double y, double z)
    return Math.Sqrt(x * x + y * y + z * z);
```

8.2.6 Creating an argument around string data type

This example provides a string output which displays two condition which exists for the weather if the temperature is either above or below 20 degrees Celsius. The code reflects how arguments are written for string values. Using a functional argument.

```
//Using string arguments

static string WeatherVerify(double tempC)

        string climate = string.Empty;
        if (tempC < 20.0)
                climate = "Cold";
        else
                climate = "Perfect";
        return climate;
```

8.2.7 Creating a loop to search a parameter within a table

Tables are mainly used in contexts which use data structures. There exists a number of types of ways of handling the information which exists within this format. For instance a loop might need to be used to find a value form a list. This could be within a number of formats. There might also be other attributes which exist for this format, which are also specific to the data type or parameter within the functional definition of the dot operator. The example below is to search a table of scores to retrieve the condition.

```
//Using a table within functional format

int[] scores = {97, 92, 81, 60};
// Imperative approach
var ScoreAdv = new List<int>();
foreach (var item in scores)
    if (item > 80)
                    scoreAdv.Add(item);

static Tuple<Action, Action, Action> CreateBound()
{
    int val = 0;

    Action increment = () => val++;
    Action decrement = delegate() {val--;};
    Action print = () => Console.WriteLine("val = " + val);

    return Tuple.Create<Action, Action, Action>(increment, decrement,
print);

//tests the condition of an element

public static int Count<T>(T[] List, Predicate<T> condition)
{
    int counter = 0;
    for (int i = 0; i < List.Length; i++)
    if (condition(List[i]))
      counter++;
    return counter;
```

8.3.1 Object orientated vs Functional

Unlike object orientated functional programming is mainly concerned with creating procedures which return values and modify data sets. Due to the Logical statements and conditions which exist within the style, there are differences between how these two types of programming are written. This difference mainly exists in how objects and variables are declared and also the contexts which exist within the method statements. For this reason functional programming is better suited to events which contain mathematical concepts, here the basis of procedures occur due to the differences which pertain between variables.

Despite this the format for writing; object orientated programs are often easier due to the parenthesis of statements and how logical arguments are built by the compiler. This is important to point out as the compiler is mainly responsible for interpreting the code.

DIFFERENCES BETWWEN FUNCTIONAL AND OBJECT ORIENTATED	
FUNCTION BASED	Object based
COBOLT, FORTRAIN	C+, Java
ALGORYTHMS	Data selection
PROCEDURAL	Non procedural

Table: 8.3.1 detailing the differences between the two concepts

Summary of chapter

This chapter has tried to offer an insight into a separate coding practice, which has its own form of evaluations within the compiler. Making the techniques and procedures used within functional programming different to other types of domains. Functional programming is mainly concerned with the process of creating a procedure or a function, as the means of forming a program. This means that complicated code is able to create algorithms which manipulate or form the procedure. The chapter has explored some of the differences in form by looking at how functions are used on different datatypes and attributes.

End of Chapter Quiz

Identify two concepts within functional programming?

Explain how to initialise an object?

Create a procedural function which uses a second procedure within the parenthesis?

What type of software is functional programming more suited to?

CHAPTER 9

Object orientated programming

In this chapter you will look at the following

- Definition of object orientated
- Creating an object and class
- Using abstraction and encapsulation
- Inheritance and polymorphism

9.1.1 Defining object orientated programming

Like procedural programming object orientated is a type of context used to create the methods within a program. Object orientated programming has its own set of procedures which determine the functionality of the code. There are a number of techniques used within object programming which make this form of programming different to other types of styles. The main quality of the domain is that it is able to create contexts and definitions which are used by structures and procedures within the code. Here the program defines the data types of a set of values within a class, which other procedures are able to use when calling upon the object. This means that variables have clear definitions of values, and separate objects can be created which have their own forms of data type definitions.

The main purpose of the paradigm is to declare a set of variable types within a class which the program can then use as a reference point within procedures. The example below describes a statement used to declare a set of variables.

Namespace Travel destination

Var TravelMethod = String
Var Cost = Double
Var TimeofTravel = String

Classe Travel
Public Static main

The variables defined within the namespace will be the properties give to the object. The data type determines how the properties within the object are processed by the CPU. For instance it is only possible to use string attributes for data types which use an alphanumerical code. The idea is to clearly define the parameters so that the procedures are able be parsed by other processes with the computers program.

A program can use as many types of objects as needed for the procedure to work. It is also possible to create a number of classes within a single namespace. Although it is important to separate the programme from the elements which define the objects as this effects how the procedure is read by the system during the program.

Below is a table which lists the benefits of using object orientated programming.

DIFFERENT TYPES OF SOFTWARE ALGORYTHMS	
CLEARLY DEFINE DATA TYPES	Reduces dataspace
CREATE A NUMBER OF OBJECTS	Reduces code issues
USES STATIC AND POLYMORPHISM	Map objects
HIGH LEVEL OF ABSTRACTION	

Table: 9.1.1 benefits of using object orientated programming

9.1.2 Creating a namespace and a class

A namespace is used to declare a part of the programme which will contain a class structure for the definition of objects. Any objects defined in this namespace can share definitions as set out within the variable declarations. For example creating a secondary object within the program will mean that the properties used will share the same data types as the original object. The program below identifies a typical procedure to declare the datasets within a program. The namespace designates the area of the program within which a class of data types can be used.

Namespace timetable

Var date = String
Var time = Double
Var timeofDay = String

Classe Autumn structure
Public Static main

Public Static Main()

Here the section after the namespace is used to declare the variables. The class entitled autumn structure is where any object which uses this class will appear. If needed it is possible to create a secondary class for objects, or create an entirely separate namespace for a secondary set of class definitions. This process of identifying the data types allows the procedures within the program to select the correct type of attribute or encoder. Otherwise datatypes would be misinterpreted and stall the application during runtime. Another reason this procedure is used is that attributes only pertain to certain data types. For instance parsing a sort function on a string is slightly different to a numerical version of the same function. Meaning that this process is important for the procedures to function inside the program.

9.1.3 Creating an object

Once the data types have been declared within the namespace, it is possible to create the parameters used to define an object. An object basically encapsulates the parameters used to define a process or entity within a program. The below object is the parameters used to define a rectangle. Here there are set of variables which define the rectangle, such as area, length and width. These are used to construct the object.

```csharp
using System;

namespace NewOperator {
class Rectangle

    public int length, breadth;

    // Parameterized Constructor
    // User defined
    public Rectangle(int l, int b)

      length = l;
      breadth = b;

    // Method to Calculate Area
    // of the rectangle
    public int Area()

      return length * breadth;

// Driver Class
class Program {

    // Main Method
    static void Main(string[] args)
    {
      // Creating an object using 'new'
      // Calling the parameterized constructor
      Rectangle rect1 = new Rectangle(10, 12);

      // To display are of the Rectangle
      int area = rect1.Area();
      Console.WriteLine("The area of the"+
          " Rectangle is " + area);
```

As you can see the program is used to determine the area of a rectangle which has the properties defined within the object. The purpose of defining the parameters within the object is that the same procedure can be used to declare any number of objects which have slightly different definitions. C# uses this process to create the procedure, as this is how the compiler interprets the code.

9.1.4 Initialising an object

The program above is merely the procedure which is used within the memory space to create a process. During the procedure an object needs to be created so that the item is found within a memory address. For instance the memory address for each of the sides of the rectangle need to be created as well as a memory location for the area. This process occurs within the programme during the object initialisation. This process is also referred to as the class constructor, meaning that the programme designates an area of memory which part of the programme can be stored within. For example, connotations of the same object require, two separate allocations of memory.

The following code is where the instance of the rectangle class is created

```
public Rectangle(int l, int b)

    length = l;
    breadth = b;
```

The object which is used within the programme is initialised under the following constructor.

```
Rectangle rect1 = new Rectangle(10, 12);
```

It is possible to tell when an object is initialised as the name appears twice with the value new, which designates that the recatanglerect1 is a new constructor. This means that the information which pertains to rect1 now has its own memory location.

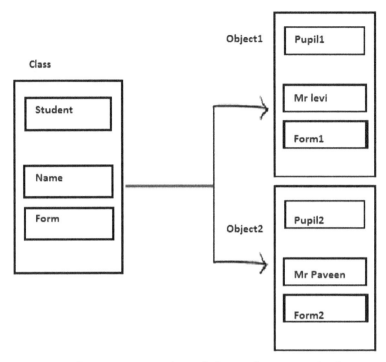

Fig 9.1.4 creating a number of objects from a single class

9.2.1 Abstraction and encapsulation

Data abstraction within object orientated programming is the process of hiding data sources form other parts of the programme. This is achieved within the domain through the clear definition of separate classes and that programmes are only able to use objects within their own clearly defined class. By using this procedure a programme is able to access the information which pertains to that particular procedure and not interfere with parts of the programme which are irrelevant to other structures within the code. This process should allow the programme a clear set of rules when defining the uses of the datatypes and variables. Using abstraction means clearly separating the terminology between points within the programme.

Encapsulation stops the code interfering with a specific object. Here the program and the object are clearly defined. The programme should be able to call the object. Although the object has its own part in the procedure, which is separate from the main programme.

9.3.1 Inheritance and polymorphism

These two definitions refer to the concept of object orientated programming; in that it is an extension to the way objects are created within classes. For instance a class might be created within a namespace so that other classes can use the declaration contained within the namespace.

The example below describes how a class can have a secondary type of definitions which use its own versions of the original variable declarations.

```
using System;
namespace Inheritance

// base class
class Animal

    public string name;
    public void display()
    Console.WriteLine("I am an animal");

// derived class of Animal
class Four Legs: Animal

    public void getName()
    Console.WriteLine("My name is " + name);

static void Main()

    // object of derived class
    Four Legs Dog= new Four Legs();

    // access field and method of base class
    labrador.name = "Retreiver";
    Dog.display();

    // access method from own class
    Dog.getName();
```

As can be seen the original declarations provided within the class for animals can be used again within the theory of inheritance to designate the secondary class dogs, where it is possible to create a number of secondary objects, which are separated from the original programme.

The second example below describes the concept of polymorphism. This is where an object is able to be called again within the program, under a different set of terms. The idea here is that the program is able to repeat the definitions used within the original procedure, and create a secondary process using the original terms. The program identifies how a single object in a program can be called depending on the type of input or expected output. Within polymorphism the code is extended to repeat process needed for the new program.

```
using System;
class Program

// method does not take any parameter
public void greet()

Console.WriteLine("Hello");

// method takes one string parameter
public void greet(name)

Console.WriteLine("Hello " + name);

static void Main()
Program p1 = new Program();

// calls method without any argument
p1.greet();

//calls method with an argument
p1.greet("Tim");
```

Summary of chapter

In this chapter we have looked at why variables are defined within objects for the use of parsing different types of attributes and parameters. Creating an object definition by declaring variables can be more efficient and allows the programmer to separate the programme from the object definitions. This form of programming is very useful when the user needs to work with a number of different sets of data types under different conditions. The chapter looked at creating and initialising an object and some contexts which are relevant to the domain.

End of Chapter Quiz

Create a namespace and declare a set of variables?

Use code to initialise a new object?

Provide an example of using more than one class in a namespace?

How does object orientated differ to other types of programming domain?

CHAPTER 10

Full Stack Programming

In this chapter you will look at the following

- The definition of full stack
- Front end and back-end programming
- Development cycle
- Applications and web development

10.1.1 What is full stack software development?

The main focus of this part has been to look at the development of software design, through providing a critique of differing software domains. The purpose of a domain is to specialise on certain procedures which are specific to a designs concept. This allows a developer to approach topics such as data processing to create algorithms which are more relevant to this type of media. The purpose of understanding domain theory is to separate areas so that the code is more relevant to the platform than across different processes. This allows the developer to use the appropriate tools to develop the software. Full stack programming is slightly different in that the entire design process is achieved within one platform. Bringing together elements of a number of different domains.

Full stack software development is the process of creating all the elements within a program or piece of software. For instance most software comprises of the user end information, which is the form data and console-based application. There are also other components to the platform such as the programming procedures and the information which is contained in data tables. Within full stack programming all these elements are added together to make a comprehensive program which comprises of a number of processes or stages. Here the programme is more than a number of pieces of code, but entire software platform.

10.1.2 Applications of full stack programming

Full stack programming has a range of applications and is used across many types of platforms including the web and within console-based definitions. Due to the concept of full stack being mostly concerned with the user interface it is a user-friendly approach to creating software. A program can be termed full stack when there are a number of layers to the program. Meaning that the user interface is just the shell in which the software is able to communicate to the programmed features, and the data structures which exist within the software. Below is a list of benefits of using this type of design.

BENEFITS USINGTHIS PLATFORM	
UTILISES MANY ELEMENTS	Understands processes
USER FRIENDLY	Comprehensive
MORE INTERACTIVE	More robust design
RELIABLE	

Table: 10.1.2 benefits of using full stack software

10.2.1 Front end and back-end procedures

As already mentioned, programming an entire application means not only creating the user interface, but also making the procedures which constitute the decisions within the program. This means that most types of software coding is specific to either of these two forms of development. Full stack means taking the elements of both kinds of processes and using these to create the entire piece of software. To development this idea further it is necessary to first point out what both elements consist of from a developers view point. The table below identifies how the two concepts differ in terms of how they are applicable to a software application.

Front End	Back End
HTML, CSS, JAVASCRIPT	PYTON, C#, SQL

The creation of user-friendly interfaces. Creating functional detail within the application	Web server processes. Interpretations of data base applications. Procedure and programming which exists within the application.
Imaginative concepts which to build the software.	Analytical and logical procedures.

Table 10.2.1 identifying the differences between front and back end

Here Front-end processes are essentially based around the user content. This might be in the form of a console application or the HTML web page which has the graphical interface that enables the user to navigate between web pages. This means that from a developer's point of view it is important to be concerned with creating a friendly and approachable interface with which to access the content available from within the platform. Such as creating the graphical indexes which highlight the points within the program, and also identifying the processes which allow them to interact with information contained within the app.

Unfortunately this text has not looked at the processes which are involved with creating the form data, and the windows user interface. This is because the text is focused more on the programming contexts which work within the design. However the process and application of front-end programming is very important as it is the part of the program which the user will have access to. The program itself will actually be locked behind the conventions of the interface, which forms the entirety of the platform for the user.

10.2.2 Creating the program within the software

The other side of the programming application consists of the information which is used to create the procedures within the code. Within the interface the user might have a number of ways of interacting with the software, such as functional buttons which are used to write code into the application and others which are used to manipulate the data. The procedures which are completed within the programme are completed within the back-end processes of the software. This means compiling the code which is able to convert the data and retrieve the information found within the programme. The programming contained in the software is very important to the functionality of the application. For this reason it relies heavily on processes which exist within certain domain theory practices, which are able to create the necessary methods and programmed procedures.

Due to the differences within the contexts of the programmable events. Front end programming uses different types of software and design routines than programming for the software internal procedures. This is due to the method and ease of creating the applications form data in languages such as HTML and JAVASCRIPT. Meaning that the two domains are often separated due to the methods of creating the procedures.

COMMON TECHNOLOGIES

FRONTEND	BACKEND	DATABASE	VERSION CONTROLS	PROJECT MGT TOOLS
HTML	PHP	MySQL	GIT	BASECAMP
JAVASCRIPT	RUBY	MANGO.DS	GRUNT	TEAMWORK
JQUERY	NODE.JS	M5SQL	SDEBUG	JIRA
CSS3	.NET		SUBVERSION	REDMINE

Fig languages used within full stack development

10.2.3 Example of a full stack design

Consider the following design for an application used for interpreting demographics. The user is able to update a spreadsheet which logs the information within a series of formats, such as the time period and data types. The software is then able to provide a report which includes the information written into the tables. The purpose of the application is to allow the user to decide how the information is presented and what parts of the data are converted within the reports. The user might also be able to communicate with other servers to add or retrieve information which can be added to the demographics. Which can be viewed graphically within a number of formats. The software must be able to provide the user with the information without the need to use any coding, meaning the interface needs to be user friendly without the need to perform the calculations. The figure below identifies a typical output for the report.

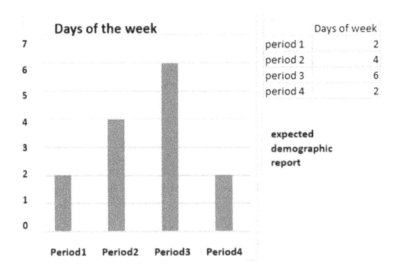

Fig 10.2.3 Example output for a demographic software

There are a number of other aspects to the software other than the interface. The program needs to create a range of statistics from the information input into the system, which includes creating the reports and graphical analysis of the information. The idea here is to decide how the parts are created and how the program is expected to develop from the possibilities of the applications purpose. For instance, a major consideration of the programme is how the data is updated within the tables. A SQL data file could be created which captured the data ready for coding. Or information could be accessed within multiple data sets and arrays, which takes parts of the data and transforms the values once the information has been categorised.

Within full stack programming the idea is complete an entire application so that all the processes are considered and the design requirements are met within the application. The reason why applications are not often seen from a full stack perspective is the differences which exist within languages used to create the different procedures. Essentially full stack programming means designing the entirety of the programme so that all parts and procedures are completed at the same time.

10.3.1 The development cycle

It is important to understand the development cycle within a software programme. As it is the key to developing a successful piece of programming software. Within Full stack programming it is expected to produce the entire finished product, which means not only making effective software but also designing a finished product which is able to cover the aspects of the designs aim. Looking at the development cycle of computer software can help produce better software applications. By applying knowledge to the design of the application before implementing and completing the project, it is possible to overcome some of the issues which occur during the design of an application, before it has started. Typically the development of a project occurs over a number of stages from analysis and design to the testing and maintenance of the finished product.

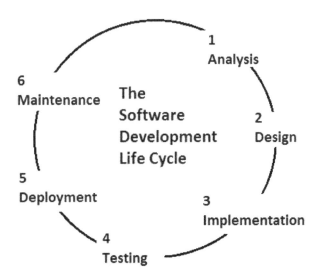

Fig 10.3.1 Diagram of the phases within the development cycle

10.3.2 Appropriation testing and design

Designing software occurs in a number of stages, through testing theories to the finished product. Design and appropriation are considered the most important stages as it is the basis for the creating the concepts which lead to the design. Appropriation testing is the process of creating the aims of the project and testing how a concept might be produced which best achieves the overall aims of the project. For instance a software design might need to be able to evaluate a number of different data types. The design of the software could achieve this in a number of ways including converting the data types, or running different procedures for each individual set of data. Obviously due to the differences which exist within the design outcomes one idea might be more suited or more appropriate to the requirements of the finished piece of software. Appropriation testing allows matching the best solution from a range of possible outcomes.

The concept to creating an effective design for an application means testing theories and working out the best approach, and looking at the needs of the design. This process helps to produce the right the code needed for the finished software

10.3.3 Testing and maintenance

Due to the many queries and procedures which might exist in a design, testing allows the code to be verified for any errors which might affect the careful running of the application. This is completed during the development phase of the program and is followed by practical maintenance of issues after evaluating the problems which developed during the design. For instance keeping the software up to date with current methods and peripherals means carefully maintaining the application and ascertaining the functionality of the project in terms of current developments in design.

10.4.1 Development of a full stack application

To explain the concept of a full stack application it is necessary to look at the types of processes which occur during the development of a programme. This can be explained using a programme for the internet. Here the design is based around the topic of a demographic for inventories which exist for an online shopping website. The website needs to explain to the owner the current stocks and sales figures from within the context of the web. This allows the user to observe information on events which occur within the website and the subsequent shipping of stock. Using this brief for a project, there exists a number of design elements which the programmer would need to take into account.

For instance the interface might take the form of an administrator log in to the site, which allows the user to have access to information which is not found on the HTML. This would be information such as stock levels and demographics on sales and where actual sales had been made. The HTML which contained this information would be written within the same document as the public website. Here there are two interfaces for the website, one which is relevant to the general public and the demographics the owners have access to.

CONSIDERATIONS OF FULL STACK PROGRAMMING

USER INETRAFCE	Domains and coding strategies
TYPES OF LANGUAGE	Data concepts
DESIGN METHODS	Network protocol
END DEISGN FUNCTIONALITY	

Table: 10.1.2 benefits of using full stack software

From a design perspective this would be considered the front end of the software. Where the two interfaces contain the relevant access to the content within the webpage. Here HTML would make the most relevant choice to create the code for the user interface. This would contain items such as current stock, and how many items are for sale. The information might be presented in the form of itemised lists which display the inventory. Designing the back end of the programme would mean creating the information needed to provide the demographics. Here the events which occur within the website need to be recorded and turned into relevant statistics. This can then be used to provide the figures to the administrator board.

Another consideration from a programming perspective. Is creating a number of data structures, which not only contain the information of the items, but also the current levels of stock which this relates to. The content of the data structure would have information on the details of products which are available, contained within a data base, which is accessible from the HTML address. Here the use and programming of data structures would be important to the content of the site.

In fact the overall programme could be achieved in any number of ways, except a number of considerations need to be considered which include the types for functionality of the product and also the language and coding used to create the processes.

Summary of chapter

In this chapter we have looked at what the term full stack programming refers to. In terms of the aims of the procedure, and the types of languages used to create the code. Unlike domain theory full stack includes processes which are not specific to a type of theory within programming. The basis of full stack is to design not only the code, but the user interface with which the user is able to access the programme.

End of Chapter Quiz

How does domain theory improve full stack programming?

Identify the user interface concept?

What kind of programming techniques are used within the layers of a software application?

Design a small application for the web?

PART 3

Creating applications

CHAPTER 11

Theory and appropriation design

In this chapter you will look at the following

- Concepts of designing software
- Types of platforms and languages
- Programming development stages
- Designing a simple software programme

11.1.1 Definitions of software design?

A wide range of electronic devices use programming in some way within the embedded chips found on the circuitry. The chips themselves contain many thousands of bytes of memory, which can be used to store binary capable of programming the system. For these reasons the concept of software design is applicable to many types of electronic systems and it is possible to improve electronic devices through the use of applying programmable definitions to the circuit. Programming is essentially creating a set of procedures which determines the state of the system. By altering the programming of the circuit it is possible to create new processes in the way it behaves or provide more dynamic responses to the environment of the machine.

The concept which is important here is the learning how to create a program that improves the functionality of electrical devices, whether this is a piece of software for a computer or a design for an embedded system. Learning adequate programming techniques improves the potential outcomes of the application. Meaning that the software which is created is better suited to the way the system is expected to behave. The text has offered an insight into the processes which the computer and chips are able to perform, in the expectation that the functionality which exists within the system is explained. For instance by understanding the differences between conditional based logic it is possible to make a system which is able to react to procedures or inputs in way where it is able to make decisions. The process depends on the hardware of the system and the functionality of the software.

To highlight this process consider the following code. Which is dependent not only on the software but also the hard ware in which it is written on.

For instance

```
IF X=> Y Condition1 ()
Else return to loop
```

```
return
```

Here the code represents a condition to compare two inputs, within a program this could be any type of event or even a location within the systems memory. Form a programmer's perspective it is not only necessary to understand the logic of the circuitry but also how the program is expected to develop in the code. The purpose of the text has been to highlight the resources available to the programmer in terms of the functionality of design, and also how the code is expected to create the procedures. The text has identified a number of ways in which a programmer could create a group of routines to perform a function.

11.1.2 The context of software design

Having looked at some of the contexts of software coding, the purpose of part three is to develop an understanding of how to develop a functioning program. The aim here is to explore some of the contexts which underpin the design of a program, and the processes involved in turning the concept into an application. The last two chapters refer mainly to the idea of creating an application which is designed to work within its own platform.

11.2.1 Different types of system, physical limitations

The text has tried to point out the importance of understanding the type of system which is being used as the platform for the software. This is due to a number of reasons, the main point being the necessity to work within the constraints of the hardware. For instance some circuitry and electronic logic will simply not work within certain constraints. As the design of the system will not allow certain types of functionality and code. For this reason writing software means looking at the platform which is being used and working with the limitations of the unit. For instance a robotic vehicle might have a number of sensors and motors which it is able to use as inputs for the system. Despite the versatility of the system, programming the vehicles movements may depend on the type of chip which is being used to implement the code. Some chips are better designed to achieve certain outputs than others.

This concept is important to software design as understanding the physical limitations within the programme will help to identify some of the practical ways of achieving the aims of the design. For instance some arithmetic units are unable to complete certain processes, meaning that the design needs to be considered for logical statements which perform byte wise operations. This is just a simple example but when you need to rely on the similarity of a range of instruction sets it is necessary to identify how the platform which is being used can assimilate the intended code. Below is a table which lists a number of different types of systems and platforms for software development.

TYPES OF PROGRAMMABLE PLATFORMS	
COMPUTER	Control systems
EMBEDDED	Automation
TFT	Programmable logic
DEVICE DRIVERS	Network

Table: 2.3.3 Types of software systems and platforms

It is possible to highlight that there is in fact a broad range of systems with which to use as a basis for developing code. There are in fact a number of systems which are programmable which include automation and visual display units. Each are governed by the processes which the hardware is able to perform and the language which the developer has chosen to use as a tool for the intended platform. At a programming level the functionality depends on the physical constraints of the hardware, and how the code is expected to achieve the intended programming.

11.2.2 Programming language

As mentioned, this is usually the decision of the developer to decide which type of assembly language is used to create the procedures. Due to most types of software being integrated from previous hard ware versions, most code is developed around a similar pattern of call procedures and GOTO instructions, which means that it is possible to use similar techniques to develop a program. The difference is understanding the type of compiler which is being used within the language. For instance assembly is quite similar to machine code, whereas C# relies heavily on the interpretations performed by the compiler to create the processes. Certain functions are unable to be contextualised outside of the use of the compiler. Although the machine language works within a similar way, working between instructions and call addresses. Meaning that developing an understanding of the compiler is important to creating the code.

Another important aspect of the language is creating the right rules and contexts within the procedures to complete the task. A problem which exists with developing code is the amount of memory space which is available for the purpose of a group of instructions. As the compiler is unable to determine how much space is needed within the group of instructions. It is important to create the correct technique for writing procedures which are better designed to compile the code.

11.2.1 Designing the functionality of the code

The term functionality refers to how the code performs and completes the intended purpose. For instance an automated vehicle might make decisions based on sensors or from assimilating previous information which it has recorded onto a log. These types of processes are used to allow the vehicle to drive without the need for a controller. The functionality of these processes or the choice of procedures used depends on a number of considerations, which pertain to the versatility of the code. From a coding perspective deciding on how the functions are expected to be performed allows the developer to create the procedures within the code. Here developing and evaluating procedural based events and making choices on how the conditions for these events are met, improves the overall structure of the program so that it is more dynamic, and designed to work without failure. Taking consideration to the functionality of the code reduces errors seen within the mapping to the device.

Functionality can be improved by working through procedures in a simplified way. The best way to start coding is to simplify the terms and work through the logical stages of the procedure. Another way of improving the functionality is to consider using frameworks which work with concepts such as object orientated code to produce types of well-structured procedures which adhere to a set of rules within the language.

Developing code framework

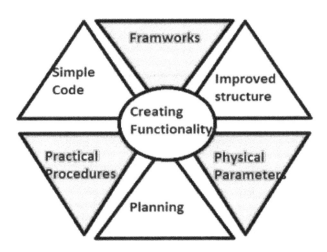

Fig 11.2.1 Developing code framework

11.3.1 Designing code

Developing a piece of software means working through a number of stages so that the code can be developed and tested before finalising the finished structure. There are a number of stages in which the process of developing the software is achieved. Such as analysing the concepts as well as working through a design procedure which covers the aims of the project. Like most designs the concept has to be investigated and an adequate solution found to the topics which the design covers. The importance of researching the topic is vital to overcoming issues which can be considered at this point within the process. Unlike other types of design software applications also need to be tested and special platforms used to manage the problems found in the initial code. However the overall process is similar to other types of design in that a concept needs to be created and tested.

Software Development process

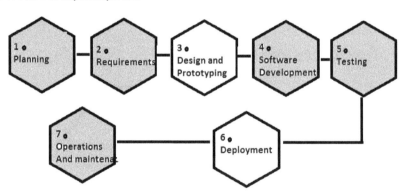

Fig: 11.3.1 Flowchart for software development process

11.3.2 Appropriation testing

This is a process which is completed at design phase. Here appropriation of the intended design is used to provide a rank score for means testing the functionality of an intended design. For instance a product or type of software might need to include aspects such as a user interface as well as a networking capability. The idea of an appropriation test is to list the desired requirements of a program and provide a score for how well the design meets the expectations. Here the overall report is able to provide a score with which to match various designs. This allows a developer to understand how the aims are being met by particular ideas. The appropriation test can consider a range of topics to allow the best solution to be found. This is a time saving tool, this allows an idea to be tested without actually being built. Below is a table of an appropriation test.

	VERY POOR	POOR	GOOD	VERY GOOD	TOTAL
PLATFORMS	Iii	Ii			5
NETWORK	Ii	I			3
DATA STORAGE	Iiii	Ii	I		7
INTERFACE	iii	i			4
					19

Table: 12.3.2 Outcomes of an appropriation test

11.3.3 Investigating a design area

Due to the various demographics which exist on the internet it is possible to base a report on figures which already exist within a topic or field. For instance the usability of a software design has at some point been studied and reports provided on the issues which occurred after the release of the product. The idea of investigating the topic is to look at the resources which are available and explore the results of past information within an area. This can provide evidence on how to strategies the development of the project. Due to the amount of investigations which have already been made available, it is no longer necessary to produce further investigations. Information can be found on online or through resources areas like libraries.

11.3.4 Maintenance and testing

This is where the procedures which have been completed within the development and prototyping phase are tested for their accuracy before their deployment into the field. The structures here need to be tested so that platforms are able to run the same code or that errors are not found when interfacing equipment. The testing phase also considers issues which occurred during the design which need to be tested to reconcile issues found within the code. The maintenance of the project is one of the last processes within the development cycle as the software needs to be maintained for a length of time, which considers software issues after the deployment of the programme. This period extends the terms of the development process to look after issues and bug fixes once it is being used by other users.

11.4.1 Creating a small program

Consider the following program for a robotic vehicle. The vehicle is expected to get between two points within a map journey using a set of coordinates for the route. The robot is also programmed with a set of procedures which determine how the vehicle is programmed to react to alterations in the journey. The purpose of getting to the secondary point is to retrieve ordinance information such as temperature responses and altitude at selected points along the map. This details the outline of the software.

The development of the software means identifying a reasonable solution to achieving the aims of the project. Which is to programme the robot to carefully manoeuvre between two points. This could be completed in any number of ways which is able to achieve the protocols needed to complete the programme. The programme takes the form of three separate processes which the robotic vehicle needs to achieve the entire procedure, such as the manoeuvring, moving between coordinates and updating the ordinance data. The diagram below shows a diagram for the using a set of sensors for the manoeuvring of the vehicle. This is only on applicable design and details how this part of the procedure might be carried out.

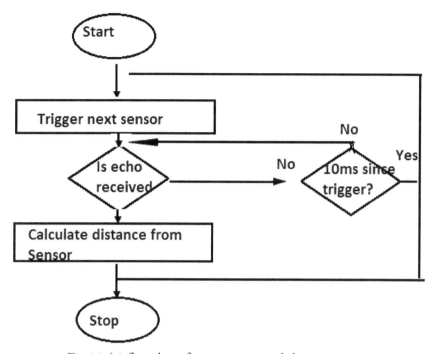

Fig 11.4.1 flowchart for an automated driving sensor

The rest of the programme is designed around the methods for storing and retrieving data when moving between the two points. This could be completed in any number of ways. Due to the way the programme is designed around inputting data from the sensors. The design of the programme should be based around a procedural format which is able to select the response form a set of instructions, depending on the place on the map or how the vehicle is responding to events in the environment. This is whether the programme would be able to coordinate the decisions. From a software development perspective there are also issues such as the application to other platforms, and the ability for the robotic to be reprogrammed to achieve other tasks if modified.

Given the design brief the task also might require a series of investigations to understand how the procedure is expected to be conducted, and how the program is expected to be tested and run in terms of a coherent timescale, which is able to effectively achieve the aims of the project. The study could also be appended to look at how this technology could be applied to other settings.

Summary of chapter

The chapter has looked at the topic of software development, which has tried to identify some of the tools and techniques that are able to improve the overall development strategy. Software design is like many other types of theory in that it uses a number of similar theories to analysis and test the concepts which meet the project goals. The main difference within software engineering is that the project needs to be constantly tested and procedures verified with new aspects of code.

End of Chapter Quiz

How does software development differ from other types of design?

What are the development stages which define how a project is completed?

Consider issues which might arise within the code?

What would a development tool be to manage the application between platforms?

CHAPTER 12

Blinking LEDS in series

In this chapter you will look at the following

- Process of creating a program
- Pin outs
- A for loop
- Adding a display

12.1.1 Definitions of software design?

In this chapter we will look at creating a simple program which can be added to a microcontroller to look at some of the processes involved while creating a simple system. For instance it is necessary to look at designing a flow chart and using a pinout table to designate the pins used for each type of output. The design of the programme is actually quite straight forward, a series of LED's are used to create a pattern by turning each diode on and off. This is achieved using a For loop which allows the program to repeat the procedure a number of times. This programme allows the use of a microcontroller to be demonstrated as well as using a TFT display to draw the outputs onto a screen. The program itself is written on a version of C# used for small systems and microcontrollers.

12.2.1 Using a flowchart t describe the programme

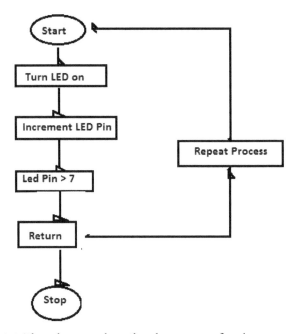

12.2.1 Flowchart to describe the process for the program

The diagram above describes the direction in which the stages of the programme develop. For instance the programme needs to turn in each diode in sequence by incrementing the pinout used by the controller, before returning to the program and repeating the process again. This fulfils the aims of the program which is to light each LED in turn so that a ripple effect is created using the diodes. The program details the start and end of the procedure and also a repeat process, which allows the program to reiterate the code.

12.3.1 The pinouts for the program

The program requires a pin output for each LED, which designates 7 pins for the series of diodes. The table below describes how the Pins are represented on the I/O of the microcontroller. This procedure allows the program to understand which pin in the port is being used within the program. Which the compiler uses to interpret the machine code needed for the code.

Input/ Output	Designation
Output 1 - pin 1	LED 1
Output 2- pin 2	LED 2
Output 3 – pin 3	LED 3
Output 4- pin 4	LED 4
Output 5 – pin 5	LED 5
Output 6 - pin 6	LED 6
Output 7- pin 7	LED 7

Table: 12.2.1 Table used to describe the pin out of the programme

12.4.1 Writing the program

The code below is what the programme uses within the microcontroller to produce the LED pattern. The For loop is used to repeat the process of the pattern, which allows the procedure to reiterate the blinking LEDS. As can be seen the declaration of the pinout occurs at the start of the program, which determines the order of the LEDS.

```
int led1Pin = 1;
int led2Pin = 2;
int led3Pin = 3;
int led4Pin = 4;
int led5Pin = 5;
int led6Pin = 6;
int led17in = 7;

int timer = 100; // The higher the number, the slower the timing.

void setup() {

// use a for loop to initialize each pin as an output:
for (int thisPin = 2; thisPin < 8; thisPin++) {
pinMode(thisPin, OUTPUT);
```

```
void loop() {

// loop from the lowest pin to the highest:
for (int thisPin = 2; thisPin < 8; thisPin++) {

// turn the pin on:
digitalWrite(thisPin, HIGH);
delay(timer);

// turn the pin off:
digitalWrite(thisPin, LOW);

// loop from the highest pin to the lowest:
for (int thisPin = 7; thisPin >= 2; thisPin--)

// turn the pin on:
digitalWrite(thisPin, HIGH);
delay(timer);

// turn the pin off:
digitalWrite(thisPin, LOW);
```

12.5.1 Creating the display interface for the LEDSs

The code below details how to program a TFT display to produce a visualisation of the outputs to the LEDS. The code is able to alter the output on the display to indicate the current sequence of the LEDs. The TFT is programmed using a case switch statement which updates the output to the display depending on the current sequence of the LEDs.

```
#include <GFX.h> // Core graphics library
#include < TFTLCD.h> // Hardware-specific library
#include <TouchScreen.h>

#define LCD_CS A3 // Chip Select goes to Analog 3
#define LCD_CD A2 // Command/Data goes to Analog 2
```

```
#define LCD_WR A1 // LCD Write goes to Analog 1
#define LCD_RD A0 // LCD Read goes to Analog 0

#define LCD_RESET A4 // Can alternately just connect to Arduino's reset pin

#define TS_MINX 120
#define TS_MINY 70
#define TS_MAXX 900
#define TS_MAXY 920

#define YP A3 // must be an analog pin, use "An" notation!
#define XM A2 // must be an analog pin, use "An" notation!
#define YM 9 // can be a digital pin
#define XP 8 // can be a digital pin

#define BLACK 0x0000
#define BLUE 0x001F
#define RED 0xF800
#define GREEN 0x07E0
#define CYAN 0x07FF
#define MAGENTA 0xF81F
#define YELLOW 0xFFE0
#define WHITE 0xFFFF

int BuzzerPin = 31; //initialise pins
int led1Pin = 51;
int led2Pin = 47;
int button1Pin = 43;
int button2Pin = 41;

tft(LCD_CS, LCD_CD, LCD_WR, LCD_RD, LCD_RESET);
TouchScreen ts = TouchScreen(XP, YP, XM, YM, 300);

void setup()
{
  Serial.begin(9600);
  Serial.println(F("TFT LCD test"));
```

```
#ifdef SHIELD_PINOUT
  Serial.println(F("Using 2.8\" TFT Arduino Shield Pinout"));
#else
  Serial.println(F("Using 2.8\" TFT Breakout Board Pinout"));
#endif

  Serial.print("TFT size is "); Serial.print(tft.width()); Serial.print("x");
  Serial.println(tft.height());

tft.reset();

uint16_t identifier = tft.readID();
if(identifier == 0x9325) {
  Serial.println(F("Found ILI9325 LCD driver"));
} else if(identifier == 0x9328) {
  Serial.println(F("Found ILI9328 LCD driver"));
} else if(identifier == 0x4535) {
  Serial.println(F("Found LGDP4535 LCD driver"));
}else if(identifier == 0x7575) {
  Serial.println(F("Found HX8347G LCD driver"));
} else if(identifier == 0x9341) {
  Serial.println(F("Found ILI9341 LCD driver"));
} else if(identifier == 0x8357) {
  Serial.println(F("Found HX8357D LCD driver"));
} else if(identifier==0x0101)
{
    identifier=0x9341;
    Serial.println(F("Found 0x9341 LCD driver"));
}else {
  Serial.print(F("Unknown LCD driver chip: "));
  Serial.println(identifier, HEX);
  Serial.println(F("If using the 2.8\" TFT Arduino shield, the line:"));
  Serial.println(F(" #define SHIELD_PINOUT"));
  Serial.println(F("should appear in the library header (TFT.h)."));
  Serial.println(F("If using the breakout board, it should NOT be #defined!"));
  Serial.println(F("Also if using the breakout, double-check that all wiring"));
```

```
    Serial.println(F("matches the tutorial."));
    identifier=0x9341;

}

  tft.begin(identifier);
  tft.setRotation(1);
  tft.fillScreen(BLACK);

  tft.drawRect(15,15,295,40,WHITE);
  tft.drawRect(0,0,319,240,WHITE);
  tft.setCursor(20,30);
  tft.setTextColor(WHITE);
  tft.setTextSize(3);
  tft.print("LED interface");

//LED heading
  tft.setCursor(30,120);
  tft.setTextColor(RED);
  tft.setTextSize(3);
  tft.print("LEDs ");

//draw BUTTON
  tft.fillRect(20,180,30,30,GREEN);
  tft.drawRect(20,180,30,30,WHITE);
  tft.fillRect(60,180,30,30,GREEN);
  tft.drawRect(60,180,30,30,WHITE);
  tft.fillRect(100,180,30,30,GREEN);
  tft.drawRect(100,180,30,30,WHITE);
  tft.fillRect(140,180,30,30,GREEN);
  tft.drawRect(140,180,30,30,WHITE);
  tft.fillRect(180,180,30,30,GREEN);
  tft.drawRect(180,180,30,30,WHITE);
  tft.fillRect(220,180,30,30,GREEN);
  tft.drawRect(220,180,30,30,WHITE);
  tft.fillRect(260,180,30,30,GREEN);
  tft.drawRect(260,180,30,30,WHITE);
```

```
pinMode(BuzzerPin, OUTPUT); //designate output pins
pinMode(led1Pin, OUTPUT);
pinMode(led2Pin, OUTPUT);
pinMode(button1Pin, INPUT_PULLUP); // designate input pins
pinMode(button2Pin, INPUT_PULLUP);
digitalWrite(BuzzerPin, LOW); //set the initial state of the pins
digitalWrite(led1Pin, LOW);
digitalWrite(led2Pin, LOW);

}

void loop()
{
  Case
    switch(digitalRead(button1Pin) == LOW) // read sensor 1
{
    digitalWrite(led1Pin, HIGH);
tft.fillRect(20,180,30,30,WHITE);
tft.drawRect(20,180,30,30,WHITE);
switch(digitalRead(button1Pin) == LOW) // read sensor 1
{
    digitalWrite(led1Pin, HIGH);

tft.fillRect(60,180,30,30,WHITE);
tft.drawRect(60,180,30,30,WHITE);

switch(digitalRead(button1Pin) == LOW) // read sensor 1
{
    digitalWrite(led1Pin, HIGH);
tft.fillRect(100,180,30,30,WHITE);
tft.drawRect(100,180,30,30,WHITE);

switch(digitalRead(button1Pin) == LOW) // read sensor 1
{
    digitalWrite(led1Pin, HIGH);
tft.fillRect(140,180,30,30,WHITE);
tft.drawRect(140,180,30,30,WHITE);
```

```
switch(digitalRead(button1Pin) == LOW) // read sensor 1
{
   digitalWrite(led1Pin, HIGH);
tft.fillRect(180,180,30,30,WHITE);
tft.drawRect(180,180,30,30,WHITE);

switch(digitalRead(button1Pin) == LOW) // read sensor 1
{
   digitalWrite(led1Pin, HIGH);
tft.fillRect(220,180,30,30,WHITE);
tft.drawRect(220,180,30,30,WHITE);

switch(digitalRead(button1Pin) == LOW) // read sensor 1
{
   digitalWrite(led1Pin, HIGH);
tft.fillRect(260,180,30,30,WHITE);
tft.drawRect(260,180,30,30,WHITE);
}
```

This code can be used to draw the display which is shown on the page below. The boxes which are under the heading LEDs, indicate which output is currently being used. The sequence of the display should match the output to the pinout of the LEDS.

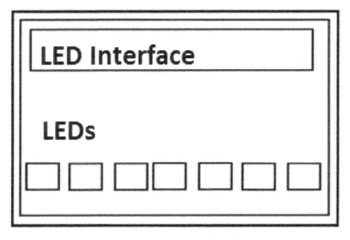

Fig 12.5.1 Display interface for TFT

Summary of chapter

This chapter has taken a small design for a program and used a number of techniques to apply this to a full design which uses and interface and set of outputs. The expectation of the chapter is to highlight the overall process involved in design and looked at some of the stages used within a program to create the overall procedure. Although the code used here is quite simple some of the stages of development are quite practical to other applications.

End of Chapter Quiz

Write a pinout table for an application?

Draw an interface for a program?

Describe the process of an application?

Design a flowchart to describe a program?

CHAPTER 13

Design of a simple program for a water station

In this chapter you will look at the following

- Process of designing a program
- Creating a design brief
- Writing a program
- Using flow charts

13.1.1 Designing a programme for a water tank?

This chapter is going to look at the design and implementation of a programme for a small automated mechanism, which is used to control the processes of the mechanics found on a water pump tower. The tower is controlled through delegating the use of two pumps to determine the amount of water found within a tank inside the tower. The water pumps are operated when the sensors detect a signal indicating high or low water. When the water level approaches the high tide mark the pumps will automatically start until the second sensor is reached, indicating for the pumps to switch off and the process to begin again. The use of this process is to automate the system of safely draining the tank without the need for a further monitoring system.

13.1.2 Flow chart to describe the water tanks mechanism

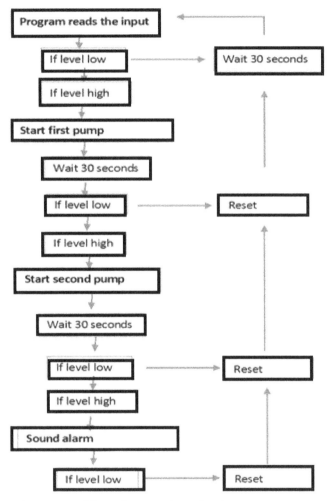

Fig: 13.1.1 Flow chart to describe the process
of the water tanks mechanism

The diagram above is a flowchart which describes the processes used within the system to control the movements of the water tank. The pumps within the water tank begins when the level reaches the first sensor which starts the process of emptying the tanks. The pump works for 30 seconds before sounding an alarm and using the second water pump. The entire process resets at any point once the low water tide mark has been reached.

The process is expected to be a fully automated meaning that manual operation is only needed within an emergency.

As can be seen the flowchart is able to visualise the processes used within the tank. Here each stage operates the pumps in turn sending out an alarm if both pumps are in use at the same time. The flowchart is used to describe each process so that it is possible to create a programme for each procedure. The flowchart also identifies how the program develops and how the program proceeds at each stage along the procedure. Creating a flowchart is a useful way of understanding how the program is expected to behave.

13.2.1 Creating the inputs and event handlers for the programme

The programme works by reading a number of sensors and running the appropriate procedure based on the information received by the programme. Here each sensor is used as a separate form of input which the programme recognises during certain stages of the procedure. Here the two sensors for the water tower are used as separate inputs 1, and 2. Which act as inputs to the program. These are used by the program to control the two outputs, which are the electrical connections used to control the pumps 1 and 2. Both input and output are designated as pins used by the microcontroller, which can be seen in the I/O connection as seen in the table listed below.

Input/ Output	Designation
Input 1 – pin 9	Sensor – water level High
Input 2 – pin 13	Sensor – water low level
Output 1 - pin 3	LED and pump 1
Output 2- pin 6	LED and pump 2
Output 3 – pin 2	Buzzer
Electrical outputs	
Input - Reset	Sensor 2 and reset

Table: 13.2.1 Table used to describe the pin out of the programme

As can be seen from the table the inputs and outputs for the programme are represented by a connection to the I/O of the microcontroller. This means that the port is able to create a response from within the programme when signals are received by the I/O. As we will see later programming the I/O designation begins at the start of the programme which starts by declaring the values of the pinouts. This is due to how the microcontroller initialises the ports before initialising the procedure.

13.3.1 Writing the program

Having created the flowchart for the program and the wiring diagram for the pin outs. It is possible to proceed with writing the code necessary to program the device. The program itself is designed around the CPU of a microcontroller. The chip is able to use the I/O port to interpret digital data received by the pins which create the event handlers required by the program. As mentioned, the pin out for the program is described at the beginning of the code. This designate which pins to the port are acting as an input or output. This is then seen as a designated event handlers from within the program.

The next part of the code is where the procedures for the pumps are written. Each stage or process of the procedure as identified within the flowchart, appear within the main struct of the program. For instance the first procedure triggers the main pump once the water level has been reached. There is also a secondary sets of commands which determine other parts of the process, including the setting of the alarm and the implementation of the secondary pump. The program below describes the entire procedure based for the water tower as described in the design brief.

```
int BuzzerPin = 2; //initialise pins
int led1Pin = 3;
int led2Pin = 6;
int button1Pin = 9;
int button2Pin = 13;
```

```
void setup()

  pinMode(BuzzerPin, OUTPUT); //designate output pins
  pinMode(led1Pin, OUTPUT);
  pinMode(led2Pin, OUTPUT);
  pinMode(button1Pin, INPUT_PULLUP); // designate input pins
  pinMode(button2Pin, INPUT_PULLUP);
  digitalWrite(BuzzerPin, LOW); //set the initial state of the pins
  digitalWrite(led1Pin, LOW);
  digitalWrite(led2Pin, LOW);

void loop()

   if (digitalRead(button1Pin) == LOW) // read sensor 1

  digitalWrite(led1Pin, HIGH); // set state if water is high
  delay (30000);
  digitalWrite(led2Pin, HIGH); // start pump 2
  delay (30000);
  digitalWrite(BuzzerPin, HIGH); // sound alarm

   if (digitalRead(button2Pin) == LOW) // read the sensor 2 for low water

  digitalWrite(led1Pin, LOW); // Turn off all mechanisms once the tank
is empty

  digitalWrite(led2Pin, LOW);
  digitalWrite(BuzzerPin, LOW);

   if (digitalRead(button1Pin) == LOW) // read sensor 1

digitalWrite(led2Pin, HIGH); // set state if water is high start pump 2

  delay (30000);
  digitalWrite(led1Pin, HIGH); // start pump 1
  delay (30000);
  digitalWrite(BuzzerPin, HIGH); // sound alarm
```

if (digitalRead(button2Pin) == LOW) // read the sensor 2 for low water

digitalWrite(led1Pin, LOW); // Turn off all mechanisms once the tank is empty

digitalWrite(led2Pin, LOW);
digitalWrite(BuzzerPin, LOW);

It is necessary to point out that from the program the procedure is created using a set of IF statements which are used to check the response from the inputs or event handlers. Here a response is needed for the I/O before moving to the next procedure within the program. There is also a series of delays which allow the program to wait while the process of using the pumps is carried out, before checking the status from the digital input or sensor.

13.4.1 Creating the interface

To improve the overall design of the software the following code is used to connect the microcontroller to a TFT interface. This allows the digital readings form the I/O port to be displayed on the TFT. This has the effect of providing a graphical interface which can be used within the tower to indicate whether a pump or sensor has in any way been triggered. The code here is an addition to the original code and has to be installed into the setup of the original pattern. What this is able to achieve is a graphical interface on a TFT display which provides the outputs for the pumps and sensors. The code is written below.

```
#include < GFX.h> // Core graphics library
#include < TFTLCD.h> // Hardware-specific library
#include <TouchScreen.h>

#define LCD_CS A3 // Chip Select goes to Analog 3
#define LCD_CD A2 // Command/Data goes to Analog 2
#define LCD_WR A1 // LCD Write goes to Analog 1
```

```
#define LCD_RD A0 // LCD Read goes to Analog 0

#define LCD_RESET A4 // Can alternately just connect to Arduino's
reset pin

#define TS_MINX 120
#define TS_MINY 70
#define TS_MAXX 900
#define TS_MAXY 920

#define YP A3 // must be an analog pin, use "An" notation!
#define XM A2 // must be an analog pin, use "An" notation!
#define YM 9 // can be a digital pin
#define XP 8 // can be a digital pin

#define BLACK 0x0000
#define BLUE 0x001F
#define RED 0xF800
#define GREEN 0x07E0
#define CYAN 0x07FF
#define MAGENTA 0xF81F
#define YELLOW 0xFFE0
#define WHITE 0xFFFF

TFTLCD tft(LCD_CS, LCD_CD, LCD_WR, LCD_RD, LCD_RESET);
TouchScreen ts = TouchScreen(XP, YP, XM, YM, 300);

void setup()
  Serial.begin(9600);
  Serial.println(F("TFT LCD test"));

#ifdef SHIELD_PINOUT
  Serial.println(F("2.8\" TFT Arduino Shield Pinout"));
#else
  Serial.println(F("2.8\" TFT Breakout Board Pinout"));
#endif
```

```
Serial.print("TFT size is "); Serial.print(tft.width()); Serial.print("x");
Serial.println(tft.height());
 tft.reset();

 uint16_t identifier = tft.readID();
 if(identifier == 0x9325) {
   Serial.println(F("Found ILI9325 LCD driver"));
 } else if(identifier == 0x9328) {
   Serial.println(F("Found ILI9328 LCD driver"));
 } else if(identifier == 0x4535) {
   Serial.println(F("Found LGDP4535 LCD driver"));
 }else if(identifier == 0x7575) {
   Serial.println(F("Found HX8347G LCD driver"));
 } else if(identifier == 0x9341) {
   Serial.println(F("Found ILI9341 LCD driver"));
 } else if(identifier == 0x8357) {
   Serial.println(F("Found HX8357D LCD driver"));
 } else if(identifier==0x0101)

   identifier=0x9341;
   Serial.println(F("Found 0x9341 LCD driver"));
 }else {
   Serial.print(F("Unknown LCD driver chip: "));
   Serial.println(identifier, HEX);
   Serial.println(F("If using the 2.8\" TFT Arduino shield, the line:"));
   Serial.println(F(" #define SHIELD_PINOUT"));
   Serial.println(F("should appear in the library header (TFT.h)."));
   Serial.println(F("If using the breakout board, it should NOT be
#defined!"));
Serial.println(F("Also if using the breakout, double-check that all wiring"));
Serial.println(F("matches the tutorial."));
identifier=0x9341;

 tft.begin(identifier);
 tft.setRotation(1);
 tft.fillScreen(BLACK);
```

```
//Print Water tower controller
  tft.drawRect(15,15,295,40,WHITE);
  tft.drawRect(0,0,319,240,WHITE);
  tft.setCursor(20,30);
  tft.setTextColor(WHITE);
  tft.setTextSize(3);
  tft.print("Water Controller");

//draw PUMP display
  tft.fillRect(180,92,40,40,GREEN);
  tft.drawRect(180,92,40,40,WHITE);
  tft.fillRect(230,92,40,40,GREEN);
  tft.drawRect(230,92,40,40,WHITE);
  tft.setCursor(30,100);
  tft.setTextColor(RED);
  tft.setTextSize(3);
  tft.print("Pumps ");

//draw SENSOR display
  tft.fillRect(180,180,40,40,GREEN);
  tft.drawRect(180,180,40,40,WHITE);
  tft.fillRect(230,180,40,40,GREEN);
  tft.drawRect(230,180,40,40,WHITE);
  tft.setCursor(30,188);
  tft.setTextColor(WHITE);
  tft.setTextSize(3);
  tft.print("Sensor");

void loop()
  if (digitalRead(button1Pin) == LOW) // read sensor 1

  digitalWrite(led1Pin, HIGH); // set state if water is high
    tft.fillRect(180,92,40,40,WHITE);//Change display
    tft.drawRect(180,92,40,40,WHITE);
    tft.fillRect(230,92,40,40,WHITE);
    tft.drawRect(230,92,40,40,WHITE);
```

```
delay (30000);
digitalWrite(led2Pin, HIGH); // start pump 2
   tft.fillRect(180,180,40,40,WHITE);//Change display
   tft.drawRect(180,180,40,40,WHITE);
   tft.fillRect(230,180,40,40,WHITE);
   tft.drawRect(230,180,40,40,WHITE);
delay (30000);
```

This provide the following interface.

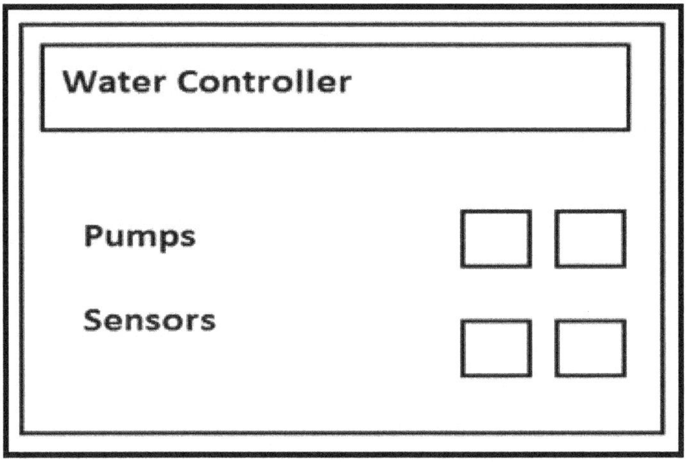

Fig: 13.4.1 Interface for water tower controller

The interface application allows the program to indicate if a sensor or pump has been triggered or is currently on. This has the effect of changing the colour of the displays button adjacent to the Pump or senor value. If the light changes colour, this indicates from within the display that the circuit is currently active.

Summary of chapter

This chapter has looked at creating a program, using tools such as a design brief and flowchart. To break the process of the program development into smaller stages. The choice of program was based around the idea of a water tower controller, which is able to use a number of inputted signals to automate the process of controlling the tanks water level. The application was also improved by using a TFT interface to display the operation of the outputs and sensors used by the device. The expectation for the chapter is to develop an understanding of the process of software applications and design.

End of Chapter Quiz

Are programs written on embedded systems considered software design?

Name a number of tools available which can be used to design programs?

Name two languages used in software design?

Describe the process of adding a display to the design?

www.ingramcontent.com/pod-product-compliance
Lightning Source LLC
LaVergne TN
LVHW041205050326
832903LV00020B/470